Mary ♡

Most Beautiful and fun
neighbor I could have
wished for! To all the
unravelling & ravelling up!
♡ Love
Camilla

Unravelling

discovering
our true selves
in midlife

CAMILLA JOUBERT

Tellwell Talent
www.tellwell.ca

ISBN
978-1-77302-662-6 (Hardcover)
978-1-77302-663-3 (Paperback)
978-1-77302-662-6 (eBook)

Table of Contents

Acknowledging

MY CONTRIBUTORS AND EDITORS

For Holly, you inspired me to be bigger than I believed possible.

Holly Kulak, Editorial and Brand Director of WeekendSherpa.com

Thank you to the insightful editors: Carrie Schmidt, Dr. Kyla Elizabeth Sentes and Robyn Matthew and the team at Tellwell as well as the endless enthusiasm of Rachel Sentes at gal-friday publicity and to Ahram Lee for her early renditions of the book cover. Special thanks to my beautiful mother Ruscilla Joubert who helped me tremendously through the process with love and encouragement. To all the writers who chose to be published and to those who were not ready to share publicly - you are all brave and vulnerable to have shared your stories of unravelling with me and with women who need to know they're not alone. And lastly to poet Oriah Mountain Dreamer for granting permission to reprint her magnificent poem "The Invitation".

Prologue

CAMILLA JOUBERT

When the idea of writing a book for women experiencing midlife crises first came about, I was still in the midst of my own three-year crisis. It had been a hefty emotional experience, and after two years of therapy involving seriously deep introspection, I began to feel like I could move forward in my life in a healthy way. But then came year three and the suicide of my brother. Between my own personal crisis, a demanding family life with young children, the tragic loss, and a sister whose life had so derailed that she had ended up in a psychiatric ward, my life was spinning out of control. Had it not been for the platform of writing to help me understand myself, there is no way I would have survived the year. As my beautiful yoga teacher Kim Boyd said so perceptively, "let 'darkness' be the teacher in the room." This resonated so much with me; the darkness of my experience taught me courage, resilience, and acceptance of my deep vulnerabilities.

As my own contribution to this volume explains, when I'd sought out resources for women of my age group experiencing midlife crises, I'd found available information to be particularly wanting. No one was talking about it, as though it was a dirty little secret to be kept hush-hush behind closed doors. I started a dialogue with my peers, many of whom had vaguely hinted at reaching crisis points in their own lives, and slowly the idea formed of creating a collection of stories and experiences.

I was encouraged by an editor friend to pursue the project and ultimately set a goal for myself to make it happen. I began actively seeking out women, between the ages of thirty-five and fifty, to share their varied stories. At the same time, a number of women began approaching me to share their experiences as well. While each writer approached the task in their own way, I set out a number of questions to help them begin the writing process. I asked them to think about when the crisis first began to manifest itself, how they felt, what impact it had on their lives and relationships, and how they set about dealing with it.

Not surprisingly, the process took much longer than I ever expected, mostly because putting such intensely personal experiences and emotions down on paper is extremely difficult for people. There's also the fact that reopening a chapter of your life you'd thought closed can unearth whole parts of your history that you thought were just that— history! But the end result has, I believe, been well-worth the wait.

While the experiences detailed in these pages are vastly different, they each share the commonality of representing a major transitional phase in the lives of these women. Some found that their crises were precipitated by major life events—like Maryanne's tragic loss of her husband or Deborah's development of a chronic illness. And some crises themselves resulted in major life changes. Nowhere is this more evident than in Casey's case, where a culmination of events allowed her to reveal and accept a part of her identity she had long kept hidden.

Others experienced more simmering and gradual dissatisfaction with their lives, like Kathi and Teresa. For L. Fletcher, the brewing storms pushed her to admit to the existence of unwelcome truths about herself and the life she had created. And some stories represent less moments of crisis than of introspection and insight into aging as a woman—like those of Nancy, Esther, and Pommy—but I believe they are just as valuable in what they have to teach us as readers. The outcomes of their experiences range from the subtle to the dramatic, and I am grateful for the honesty of writers like Trish, who was willing to share her experience of a near affair, that ultimately led her to leave her marriage, even though it cannot have been easy to do so.

Checking in on our feelings is the greatest kindness we can do for our bodies and our minds. It is neither indulgent, nor selfish. The women who wrote down their stories for this project have all been brave enough to explore their emotions and braver still to bring them to a wider audience. I truly honour the women who were courageous enough to talk to me about their feelings and share their stories with a larger audience.

The Gen-Ager

KATHI CAMERON

If I were to give a twenty-something woman advice on aging (as if I even cared about aging when I was that age) I would say: Start preparing now. If I'd known then what I know now, I would have worn more hats. I would have lathered myself in SPF 2000 and never spent one minute in the sun. I would never have started drinking red wine, because let's face it, there's no stopping now. I would have managed my stress better and would have duly noted that nachos and cheese are not included in the food pyramid. But of course, I didn't follow the advice of my much more knowledgeable older self, did I?

I did not follow the path most-travelled in my life. I married early, divorced early, began university at twenty-four, and chiselled away at an undergraduate degree until the age of thirty-two (repeating the process in grad school until I reached the ripe old age of forty). I never had children, stayed single during my thirties, and above all, rarely gave a thought to my age. I never felt my age got in the way of my professional or personal success. Perhaps it was because I was one of the lucky ones who'd held on to my youthful looks a lot longer than I deserved. Beyond exercising every day and getting my eight hours of sleep, I'd never put any effort into maintaining it. It was something I took for granted—that aging was something that happened to other people.

And as my fortieth loomed ever closer, I had a vision of celebrating the birthday with a group of my closest friends in the big city of New York (yes, just like an episode of one of those girls-in-the-city shows). Taking on the world as independent, fabulously dressed women, drinking pink martinis on a patio overlooking Central Park. Instead, I celebrated with my cat in a mobile home located in the backwoods of a small town, cake in one hand and bottle of wine in the other. I had left my beautiful city for a man who turned out to be one of the biggest man-babies I have ever known. I was now single (save for my American Shorthair—cat, that is) surrounded by various and sundry single gal paraphernalia: candles; fashion magazines; and self-help books. For the first time, I felt I had nothing to show for my life save my two degrees and a collection of handwritten journals detailing my bad choices in men and my weight loss goals for the year.

Now nearing forty-five, forty looks young, of course. I am trying to embrace my muffin top by patiently waiting until it's large enough to serve as a shelf for my drink. I would love to believe that forty is the new thirty, but let's face it...that catchphrase was invented by aging Gen X-ers desperate to hold on to their youth—a psychological life preserver. Now we have aging celebrities spending every waking hour devoted to fighting the aging process with marathon workouts and teeny-tiny meal plans combined with African elephant placenta and ancient mud from the Dead Sea to keep them looking youthful and vibrant in the magazines (thanks in no small part to the magic of Photoshop). It used to be that once a woman hit forty, they could finally breathe a sigh of relief, pack away the beauty regimens and enjoy a life of afternoon cocktails and elastic waistband pants. But the pressure to maintain our youthful good looks and sexy silhouette seems greater than ever. Of course, there are the 'pro-agers', women who supposedly "embrace their age." And sure, I appreciate looking at Julianne Moore and thinking there's hope for me—but I don't have a team of beauty experts on my payroll, or those cheekbones. Do I pay through the unaltered nose for beauty creams and anti-wrinkle cures promising the reversal of time? Of course I do. To me, anti-wrinkle cream is like prayer: you don't really know if it will work, but why take chances?

When I hit forty, time did start to catch up with me a bit, and I realized that if I wanted to fit into the same size pants I had when I was thirty (not twenty, which would clearly just be wishful shrinking), I was going to have to change my eating habits. I learned to eat more veggies and less processed food. I limited my wine intake (sort of), and exercised in moderation. The fact is, once you hit forty, exercise doesn't have the same impact on your body as a sound nutritional plan. So, over the course of the next four years, I made the necessary changes to my diet and physical activity and lost twenty pounds.

I was starting to feel like things were on track; I had a great career, a great man friend, and a great social network. Then, at forty-three, I heard it for the first time, that well-meaning punchline that feels like a kick in the proverbial muffin top: "You sure look great for your age."

Yep, I was 'officially' middle-aged.

How the hell did this happen to me? I honestly never thought it would. But sure enough, here it is. Every morning, I review the effects of aging in the mirror, pulling my jowls back to reveal the woman I remember. I can handle the new wrinkles I see forming under my eyes. I can handle the change in my jawline. What I cannot yet bring myself to accept is the form my neck is starting to take (something resembling a slouch sock), and the wrinkles that liken my chest to a topographical map. No one ever told me I'd have chest wrinkles—or even that such a thing existed!

I'd always been quick to say that people who experienced the purported 'midlife crisis' just lacked the self-awareness and courage to 'pursue their bliss' in their twenties; they were doomed to suffer an existential panic attack as the years rolled on. Whereas I, on the other hand—who had pursued my career goals and achieved my academic dreams—was confident that I would never experience any regrets or disillusionment. That was, until I hit the middle-age mark myself.

Over the past few months, a wave of life-challenging questions has washed over me. I have questioned my life choices and started to regret some of the paths I have taken. Have I actually reached my full potential? Or do I have more to look forward to? Do I want to continue to pursue my career? Or would I be happy with a simple life centered around a vegetable garden? Should I have been a lawyer? Or maybe a Vegas showgirl? Should I have moved to a larger city, one with countless opportunities, instead of moving to a rural area for a relationship that was doomed from the beginning?

I do now enjoy the benefits that come with committing to a profession for over twenty years. I feel confident saying that I am an expert in my field and can make a difference in someone's life by plying my craft. I am known for what I do, and have a strong reputation within my community. But is that all there is? Where do I go from here? What am I going to do for the roughly twenty-one years I have remaining in my profession?

Why am I asking so many questions?

While there is nothing anyone can do to stop time, and the alternative is none too appealing, I believe my aging ego is in desperate need of an attitude makeover. How do I define myself as I move to get friendly with fifty? Where do I fit in the world? What positive contributions can I make during this transition?

One of the benefits I can see in having a midlife identity crisis is the opportunity it offers for change. If we can take enough time to really address those challenging questions, we can take the necessary steps to create a life that just may exceed our twenty-something expectations. Many of us however, are juggling diminishing energy levels, family, job and relationship. There's not enough time in the day for that kind of introspection. And God forbid, we ask the questions and don't like the answers. God forbid we uncover a deep sadness that can only be relieved by abandoning our life to pursue some previously unrecognized 'true' calling (though I doubt there is a great demand for forty-something Vegas showgirls).

But change, any kind of change, can result in a sense of loss. Some losses are bigger and have greater impact than others, but all loss can produce sadness. I am losing my youth, ever so slowly, like a silent film star choking out her last lines. I cannot help but wonder how old I really look, and where that leaves me. And one prospect that really scares me, is that whole 'change of life' thing. From the hairs growing in places they shouldn't, to increasingly sleepless nights and those lovely 'hot flashes' I hear all about.

How can I 'look forward' to vaginal dryness? What does that even mean? I can admit that I stay up nights thinking how unfair it all is...or maybe it's those changing hormones that are making it almost impossible for me to sleep? Although I hate the fact that I lose sight of my ankles once a month, and experience cramps that almost make the argument for a complete hysterectomy, I'm going to miss it when it's gone. The monthly suffering serves almost as a symbol of my youth: I haven't dried up yet! Then there's the horrific double-standard of aging, because what happens to our opinions of men as they reach midlife? They improve! They get sexier. And they certainly don't apologize for the dimples on their fifty-year-old asses.

As I contemplate my future, I feel like I have two choices. I can try to fight the biological signs of aging with strict diets and exercise regimes, coupled with skin care treatments and maybe the odd dermabrasion, I can continue to identify through my appearance, leading me to a near panic attack each time I walk past a car window, only to realize that you really can't fight against the passage of time. Or I can stand up and learn a better form of self-acceptance even when I'm wrinkly and bent over like a question mark.

No one has ever had inscribed on their tombstone: "Beloved wife and mother who looked great for her age." Having a lasting impact is being remembered as someone who cared for others and gave back to her friends, family, and community. So bottom line is I'm going to have to pull my head out of my face cream and stop pining for the good old days of smooth skin, shiny hair, and the ability to eat the entire cake without gaining a pound (not that I'd know anything about doing that).

To that end, I have created a few long-term goals for myself that don't include fitting into my twenty-something jeans or saving for plastic surgery. I believe it is important for women to continue to challenge and reinvent themselves. Education has always served me well; there's something about the pursuit of knowledge that keeps me energized and inspired. So now, as I plan my second graduate degree in counselling psychology, I look towards my future and feel a sense of excitement. By fifty, I intend to open my own centre for health promotion; the goal has renewed my sense of purpose and passion. No matter how old you are, happiness today is the product of hope for tomorrow.

The continuous pursuit of our passions will keep us energetic, happy, and hopeful—no matter our age.

The reality is that I will most likely continue to practice random acts of vanity as I get older, but I will try my best to do so with a lighter heart. I will connect with those who support me and make me laugh, and will walk away from those who don't. I will try my best to get my eight hours of sleep a night, eat my veggies, and go out for a daily walk. I will laugh often, and love much, but no matter what happens...I will never dance naked in my living room (like no one's watching).

Post-script

Since I first wrote this essay I turned forty-six, and I've realized that at some point along the line I suddenly stopped fretting about the wrinkles and started to appreciate everything I have in my life. It finally became apparent that I wouldn't trade my muffin top, grey hairs, or wrinkles for another chance at youth if it meant giving up what I have gained and learned so far. I guess that is the wisdom that comes with aging (or with the realization that there is nothing you can do to stop it). I'm not saying I have this aging thing in the bag, but it's a step in the right direction.

The Path with a Heart

MARYANNE POPE

"I believe we have two lives," Glenn Close tells Robert Redford in *The Natural*, "the life we learn with and the life we live after that."

Perhaps what we call the "midlife crisis" is the dividing line between the two. If so, then I can pinpoint the precise moment I passed from one to the next: 5:53 a.m. on Friday, September 29th, 2000. That's when my husband, John, a police officer, fell to his death. John was investigating a suspected break and enter complaint at a warehouse when he stepped through an unmarked false ceiling and fell nine feet into the lunchroom below. There was no safety railing in place to warn him of the danger.

The back of John's head struck the concrete floor at such an angle and with such force that he suffered a massive brain injury. Within hours, he was declared legally brain-dead. John was thirty-two. So was I.

There had been no intruder in the building. It was a false alarm. The impact on my life of that call, however, was devastatingly real. For while John lay dying on that lunchroom floor, I was at home in bed, tossing and turning, furious with myself for not having gotten up when my 5:00 a.m. alarm had rung. I'd promised myself the night before I'd wake up early and do some writing before going in to my regular job.

Becoming a writer had been my life's dream. The necessity of actually *working* towards achieving said dream hadn't quite hit home.

Yet.

So what was it that had prompted me to make this promise to myself—the one I hadn't kept—on that fateful Friday? It had been an argument with John...and it had been a doozy.

We'd been at the dog park on Thursday afternoon, trying to clear the air after John having given me the silent treatment for the prior three days over my apparent unwillingness to say 'no' to my mother's unreasonable demands on my time, demands that were hindering my writing aspirations. I thought he was being an immature jerk for choosing silence as his form of communication.

"I'm so scared," I blurted out to John at the off-leash park that Thursday afternoon, "of waking up twenty years from now and still not have finished writing a book."

He'd stopped walking, turned to me and said, "You're probably right about that, Maryanne. Just as long as you know that will have been your choice."

My mouth dropped open. How dare he? I thought we were trying to make up!

But he had more to say. "Until you make your writing a priority, nobody else will."

That was our last conversation. He went to work that night and never came home again.

The next time I saw him was in a strangely inactive emergency room. John was unconscious, lying on his back on a stainless steel gurney and draped in a white sheet. I didn't know that the medical staff had already given up trying to save him and had instead moved on to stabilizing his body in preparation for organ removal.

I ran up to him, grabbed his hand, kissed him on the lips and whispered, "John, I love you!"

No response. The silent treatment had been reinstated. But this time, it was permanent.

Although John never made it home again, he had tried to come see me, just a couple of hours before his shift was to end. I found this out several months after his death when I went out for dinner with Lil, the police officer he'd been working with the night he fell. Lil went through the printout from their shift with me, which essentially gave me a play-by-play of the last hours of John's life.

"We were on our way to your place to see you that morning," Lil said, "when another call came in and we had to take it."

"What time?" I asked.

She ran her finger down the printout. "About 5:00 a.m."

"But I wasn't supposed to go in to work until 7:00 a.m.," I said. "Why would John be coming home so early to see me?"

Lil shrugged. "I don't know. You tell me."

I hadn't told John about my promise to wake up early and do some writing before going into work. But then it hit me—I didn't have to. He knew me better than I knew myself. Since we are creatures of habit, John would've known that after our fight on Thursday afternoon, I would have resolved to smarten up and start taking my writing seriously. I would have promised myself to wake up early the next day. Then I would proceed to ignore the alarm, roll over and go back to sleep. Then I would beat myself up over it and then try again the next day.

Under normal circumstances, this pattern of procrastination-guilt-procrastination would repeat itself. It wasn't new. So John was likely coming home to make sure I was awake and keeping my promise to myself. But since he didn't make it back, his death woke me up instead.

Message received.

And so began my second life, after the one we "learn with." But this second life is not devoid of learning opportunities. On the contrary, in my experience it is chock-full of it. The difference though, is that it is far more focused learning, because we are, at long last, in the driver's seat of our own destiny—even if it is hell we're navigating ourselves through. Whereas in that first life we are more like passengers looking out the window, taking it all in, dreaming of what we'll do with our lives when the day comes where we're in that coveted position of driver.

Then, when 'one day' comes, which it always does—though thankfully not necessarily cloaked in tragedy—it is as if our soul awakens from its slumber and we finally 'get it': our time here is finite. It will end. And we realize we really only have two choices: 1) continue to live the life others expect of us, or 2) live the life we are here to live.

So if we choose the latter, how do we know we're on the right path— *our* path? I've found this passage from Carlos Castameda helpful to me: "A path is only a path, and there is no affront, to oneself or to others, in dropping it if that is what your heart tells you...Look at every path closely and deliberately. Try it as many times as you think necessary. Then ask yourself alone, one question...Does this path have a heart? If it does, the path is good; if it doesn't it is of no use."

Through all the heartache and the hurt, the hard work and the challenges, the pain and the setbacks, the sorrow and the roadblocks, I think we are on our path when we know that at the end of it all— whenever that may be—we will die a happy and fulfilled person who has achieved what we set out to do. And, if we avail ourselves of the opportunities around, a heck of a lot more. For as difficult as it was for me to admit and accept, the truth is that John's death afforded me tremendous opportunities. Because he died in the line of duty, I am entitled to receive his paycheque for the rest of my life. For a writer, this is a dream come true. For a woman who has just buried her soul mate, not so much.

Two weeks after John's death, I sat down at my computer and started writing the manuscript that would become my first book, *A Widow's Awakening*. It would take me eight years to get the manuscript where it needed to be, let alone get *myself* to where I needed to be in order to share such an intensely personal story. For as I would soon learn, the personal process of grieving is a full-time job in and of itself. Sharing one's grief with the public takes the process to a whole other level. Throw in the complications that come with learning how to write *well*, and trying to determine how best to tackle the issue that started the whole nightmare in the first place (workplace safety), then actively engaging with the issue through public education, and you've got a gal with an awful lot on her plate.

In my humble opinion, workplace safety was clearly an issue that needed to be better addressed. Thankfully, I wasn't alone in my understanding of the preventable nature of John's death. Shortly after he passed away, several of his fellow police recruits started the John Petropoulos Memorial Fund (JPMF). They asked me if, at some point, I'd like to be involved in how the funds were used. I said yes.

More than a decade later, the JPMF is a registered charity that raises public awareness about workplace safety issues facing emergency responders. The fund's five, thirty-second, public service announcements have aired on TV over half a million times. The powerful 10-minute safety video, *Put Yourself in Our Boots* (also created by the fund), is being shown in safety meetings, presentations, and conferences across North America.

However, the fact of the matter is that by choosing to become a workplace safety advocate on behalf of one's dead husband, it tends to lessen one's chances of finding a new one any time soon—at least, in my experience. Perhaps my involvement in the field is perceived as holding on to the past. I, however, prefer to see it primarily as a way of using the past to prevent future tragedies. But it's undeniable that the sheer amount of time, effort, love, and money it takes to do all this meant that time, effort, love, and money were spent *not* doing what most of our friends were doing in their mid-thirties: raising families.

Because of the public nature of John's death and the immense support network we had in place, all of the above took place inside a goldfish bowl with dozens of people constantly tapping on the glass. At first, people were just trying to make sure I was alright (and overfeeding me) but their compassion soon shifted towards questioning what I was going to do with my life. They'd advise me to go back to my old job or find a new one, reminding me that, at some point, I had to "move on" (read: fall in love again, get married and have a baby or two) and *then* all would be well again.

But for *whom*?

John and I hadn't gotten around to the child portion of the program. At the time of his death, I had been on the fence about the motherhood matter, feeling I needed to become a writer first. However, there is a significant difference between making the parenthood decision with one's spouse versus having the decision being made for you by something as mundane as a missing safety railing.

And while my midlife crisis was precipitated by tragedy, the end results all boil down to the same thing: you not only make a choice as to how you are going to live your life moving forward, you also, eventually, learn to accept the sacrifices that come with that decision.

But that doesn't mean everyone else around you is going to be on the same page. That is where I found the path got particularly tricky to navigate. It is very difficult to try and listen to the soft whispers of one's heart and soul when the mortals around you are screaming far louder to be heard. In all fairness, the people around me wanted to see me return to the person I *used* to be.

But at 5:53 a.m. on Friday, September 29th, 2000, *everything* changed. The moment John fell to his death, I too, began a freefall into a new life, forcing me to face all the changes that accompanied not only widowhood, but midlife as well.

So where did I go to find the necessary peace and quiet to begin to find my path? Where my heart rested, of course: John's grave. Except that it wasn't just his grave; it was also *mine*—literally. While John's destiny was now physically carved into that stone, mine was still a blank. At thirty-two, I knew exactly where I was going to end up—I just didn't know when. And despite the horrific hurt that comes with 'hanging out' with my husband's headstone, instead of him, it was very conducive to helping me face my own mortality and what that meant for my journey.

Fast-forward a decade and the day came when I finally found the courage to leave my chaotic life in Calgary. For the number of people tapping on my little goldfish bowl had not only significantly increased, so had the intensity of the taps.

I had achieved what I'd set out to do after John's death, and more. At forty-two, I knew the time had come to fulfill my other dream: being a writer by the sea. So I sold my Calgary house, packed my belongings, moved to the West Coast, and found a cute little bungalow that suited my new life as a single woman with two senior dogs.

Now I am forty-four. It has been nearly twelve years since John died and I am truly living the life I want. I am finally at peace with not having a child—my own, adopted, foster, or otherwise. This peace, however, hasn't come from 'accepting' reality. Rather, it came from years of struggling over the decision of whether or not I wanted to be a mother and finally arriving at an answer. I always knew that if motherhood was going to happen, the magic age it would have to happen by for me would be forty-three.

Now that I've arrived at the other side of that number, I am profoundly grateful I didn't have a child. In the end, the decision came down, again, to choosing the path of passion, and my heart simply wasn't in motherhood.

I look at my days now and they are exquisite in their simplicity and purpose. John's belief in my potential as a writer inspired me to write. His life taught me about the hard work and determination necessary to achieve one's dream. His death gave me the financial means to become the best writer I can be and gave me the freedom to live where I want.

Although I don't have John to share my path with, I do have his love and the lessons learned from his life and death. As such, I am making full use of the life I learned with, as I continue to move forward with the life I'm now living.

Keeping the Beast of Midlife at Bay

POMMY

"A life without cause is a life without effect"
- DILDANO IN *BARBARELLA, 1968.*

So, what exactly *is* a midlife crisis?

Honestly, I don't have a clue. As forty approaches it seems to me that it's something that is supposed to be looming on the horizon for most women—but it really hasn't materialized for me in any traditional sense. Don't get me wrong, I'm not complaining. But it does feel a bit like a sword of Damocles hanging over me, to think that it might be imminent. However, the more I think on it, the more I think that I've been spending a large part of my life in recent years unconsciously keeping the beast at bay, trying to mitigate the damages of a potential crisis. Because the reality is that this time in a person's life is always going to be complicated, always going to be fraught with crises; we have families and responsibilities now that have dramatically altered our existence and shifted our priorities, so how could it be otherwise? So I suppose mine is not so much a story of a midlife crisis, but rather of crises occurring in midlife.

I am a mother to three young boys, and am also a wife. My boys are seven, eight, and ten. My husband works in another city, six hours away, and comes home for weekends. How does this make me feel? Admittedly I have a little more wine these days. But don't be mistaken— I am proud to be a mother and wife. However at times I feel the title "Slave and Punching Bag" is more appropriate. It's true. My eight-year-old once asked me, "When I grow up, Mom, will you still be my slave?" I definitely gave him some food for thought with that remark!

Sure, my husband and I have had our challenges along the way. We've gone through four major upheavals which, while in some ways were very good at getting us to look at our priorities and cut out the dead wood, were also disheartening; it was heartbreaking to watch the man I love constantly get knocked back and have to pick himself up again and again. I used to try and hold it all together on the homefront, hide my stress in order to make the environment for him and the kids as normal as possible. But two immigrations, three young children, and my only family support living 12,000 miles away didn't always leave me feeling 'normal'. I would often call my mom in floods of tears when he left after the weekend—evidence that my efforts to 'keep it together' were actually tenuous at best.

The thin line I was treading probably revealed itself best whilst living in South Africa in 1996. Driving through heavy rush hour traffic I was attempting to merge onto the highway. I was honked at by the taxi driver behind me, who evidently was upset by my yielding to the oncoming hoard of cars. I responded rather loudly with expletives that unfortunately precipitated a very unexpected result. To my utter horror, the taxi driver leapt from his vehicle and within seconds was at my window, brandishing a loaded gun which he was pointing at my head. In retrospect I'm amazed I was so damn calm and collected while trying to defuse such an incredibly dangerous situation. I burst into a profusion of apologies and, in the calmest voice possible, asked him if he really thought I could manoeuvre my small car onto the insanely fast-moving traffic of South Africa's highways at breakneck speed. People have asked me if I was afraid for my life, but I wasn't afraid. I was angry at the audacity of him wielding his gun in my face, trying to intimidate me into merging more quickly. Having survived the altercation, it struck me as the perfect example of how I was playing a role in propelling my own crises. No question that he was at fault, but still, I knew better than that. And ultimately, the experience helped galvanize our decision to immigrate to the UK. We'd initially thought it would be a short-term relocation, that we'd come back after a couple of years, when things settled down in post-apartheid South Africa. I never thought I would be in the UK with my family for ten years! The move there represented a positive change for us in terms being calmer than where we'd been living, but life was certainly not much more 'settled'.

People throw around the term 'crazy' rather freely these days, but it's actually a pretty apt description of what my life is like with three boys. I spend my life in the car and sometimes even entertain the thought of actually having morning coffee with my friends in there—it's a far more feasible option! We have had so many accidents during sports, on playgrounds, and at friends' homes that the hospital staff know all our kids' names and we no longer have to fill out the forms when we arrive in the emergency room.

When my oldest boy was in hospital with an ear infection and was diagnosed with learning issues, it set the stage for another potential moment of crisis in my midlife. In fact, all three of my children have some form of auditory difficulty, attention deficit, and issues around understanding social cues. I was going insane with the slow wheels of the medical system and bureaucracy associated with the supposedly glorious British National Health System. I felt helpless for a long time and could easily have mired myself in self-pity and let the situation spin out of control, but I persevered and I learned to lean on others.

Of all the lessons my midlife years have taught me, the importance of asking for help is amongst the greatest. I would phone my girlfriends in desperation, feeling hopeless and frustrated as to how to get my sons the help they needed. And I found myself wishing for voodoo dolls to stab each time I came across someone who was completely uneducated about learning disorders, but always had a lot to say. I wanted to tear my hair out when faced with the stigma attached to my children—all unique, bubbly, and charismatic boys—as well as to my husband and I as parents. My girlfriends would listen and just let me vent and slobber on their shoulders. Without them as my rocks, I don't think I would have managed as well as I did without having a complete mental breakdown. My girlfriends are like soul sisters and they understand the demands of being a wife and a mother. I eventually also found a fantastic therapist who could give us tools to help with the auditory processing, and psychologists who taught my boys coping skills.

I have also learned the importance of leaning on that most important resource, my husband. Too often we forget that our significant other is our *partner* in this journey. My husband and I just celebrated our sixteenth wedding anniversary, although we've been together for twenty-six years. We met as young high school students, and I knew then, as I know now, that he is my soulmate. He is a brilliant dad and we miss him dearly during the week when he's away from home. He's more of a realist than I am and he helps keep me grounded. I can be very spontaneous and often want to jump right into things without thinking about the details or consequences of my actions (I'd say the gun incident falls firmly into that category). He helps me to see the big picture. He is calm, makes me laugh at myself, and can be bloody funny, too! In a crisis he is sensible, reassuring, and far more democratic than I.

I began to feel the inklings of another impending crisis a few years ago; I was feeling frustrated, directionless, unfulfilled. Now granted, my memory is not what it used to be, my body is not what it used to be, but—dammit—I feel like I'm twenty! In my mind, I can conquer the world. But I couldn't help wondering where my 'get up and go' got up and went! It was just suddenly...not there. Where was that woman who could dust off the doldrums and get on with things?

That feeling that I was spending my days carting the kids back and forth between schools and activities like a chauffeur was starting to overwhelm me. Of course, seeing them become awesome, independent, and confident people is very rewarding. Yet, I also knew that as they were growing, they were beginning to need me less and less. What was I going to do when my nest was empty? Pat myself on the back for doing such a fabulous job? Would I really be ready for the all-amazing 'me' time? For a while, I thought I could stave off the nagging emptiness with 'busyness'. I started running an art club at the local primary school. I started painting animal skulls (a bit weird, I know), all in an effort to diffuse my frustration and allow my creative self to come out and play. The fact remained, however, that making myself busy served only to make me, well...busy! It did not make me feel less stressed and I was still avoiding the root cause of my unease.

I had given up my career as the owner of a corporate events management company to be with the boys. It was because of that that I encountered that most reliable of companions for many mothers out there: guilt. I felt guilty for not being a stronger financial partner in my marriage, and I started to wonder if I should have kept working part-time. As I began to reflect on this, all the reasons why I'd given up my career came flooding back. The fact is that my husband and I had both felt this was the right decision for our sons. I hadn't been forced in to the decision (as some women unfortunately are). I had chosen to do what felt right. And that decision still feels right.

I also accepted that while many around me are comfortable with beige in their world, I love colour and expletives and chaos and emotions—I thrive on it to a certain extent. Maybe my life is one long series of crises? I don't know. I do know that with each explosion of chaos I grab that bull by the horns and always find myself on the other side of it, having grown and learned.

I have learned to be kinder to myself, embracing 'me' time without feeling selfish or guilty. I've calmed down a bit (no more melees with gun-toting maniacs!) and embraced the mantra of "this too shall pass." Midlife shows the wrinkles on my face, but I consider them my rite of passage for a life of laughter and, yes, grimaces. Gravity's taken a toll on of some of my best physical assets, but I love my soft bits. All I can think of is what an amazing thing it has been to birth and nurture three children and still have a functioning body!

I live in Africa once again. Recently, while sipping my wine in the hues of closing daylight, I realized something worth holding on to: Even if it meant losing everything I've gained from the tears and laughter I've encountered along the way, I wouldn't change my messy, chaotic life for anything. And, a glass of wine a day keeps the midlife crisis away...

Inside Out and Outside In: I fell in love with a woman, my Anam Cara (Soul Mate)

CASEY ROSS

I never considered myself to be a lesbian. Falling in love with a woman came as a shock to everyone: my husband, my children, my parents, my friends—everyone—including me! Looking back, I realize that my midlife crisis at thirty-seven was more of an identity crisis that had been years in the making.

Truthfully, I never felt normal. I believed I was imperfect and therefore never felt good enough. Growing up, I'd always felt that somehow I had to be better than I was in order to be accepted in society. I was conditioned never to say how I really felt, and to only say things that were kind and polite, or not speak at all; these were the lessons that I understood to be true. So I withheld my opinions. I defined myself by man-made laws and sadly always fell short.

I could have rebelled more, believed in myself more, and loved myself more, but I judged myself as harshly as my parents and society did. I wanted to fit in. I allowed my parents and their beliefs—as well as society's—to exert control over me. It was my choice to believe what they'd taught me. It took me years to realize that they too were products of their conditioning.

My father was a very successful businessman who, prior to his success, had been a very hands-on father, taking me "Bundu Bashing" (off-roading) on his motorbike through the forest and calling me his "princess". He fairly quickly went from fun-loving dad to strict, scary, workaholic, and distant father. I adored him and felt I had lost him to his work. So I am certain that I sought a male figure early on.

From the beginning, the type of man I attracted was the very kind I didn't want. At sixteen, Paul came into my life, and he adored me, though for some reason I just couldn't quite reciprocate his feelings. Three years later, I betrayed him by falling madly in love with Anthony, a man ten years older, whom I married at the age of twenty.

I was young and naïve and wanted the fairy tale, and I thought I'd found my prince. Instead, I was drawn into a horror story of massive proportions. If you've seen the movie *Sleeping with the Enemy*, you'll have an idea of what I lived with. Anthony was emotionally abusive and unstable. He fell into uncontrolled rages where I feared for my life. He became a monster without the least provocation. There were times when I understood how a wife could end up murdering her husband, and in those moments I felt so sorry for the women who were jailed for doing so. Emotional abuse is difficult to extricate yourself from. I am not sure where I got the strength, but after three months I left him, and we were officially divorced after six.

Anthony had scared me to death; I no longer trusted men. For almost five years my heart would nearly leap out of my chest if I even thought I saw my first husband. I hated that just the thought of him could evoke such a huge reaction in me. The whole thing had shaken my world to its core and I wanted so badly to be over him.

Paul, my childhood sweetheart, welcomed me back. I felt so grateful and made a promise to myself never to hurt him again if I could help it. He represented safety and security at a time when I felt like a rubber duck, bobbing adrift at sea. He had been my best friend and lover at sixteen, and with him I knew there would be no more abuse.

So when he proposed after two years of dating, I accepted. I said yes: not because I was wildly, passionately in love and couldn't live without him, but because I felt that I couldn't let him down again. *He must love me so much.* How could I reject his offer? He was my best friend. We could make it work.

Looking back, I should never have agreed. Honestly, I wasn't ready. I was a wounded bird. But when he asked, I didn't have the heart to turn him down. I loved him as much as I could love anybody at that time, and he felt like home. I was determined not to fail again. After all, as my family constantly informed me, "we don't get divorced." I was the first in our family to break with that tradition.

At twenty-two years old and six months into our engagement, I became pregnant with our first child and my destiny was written. I was determined to be the best wife and mother I could. But Paul was no longer the same person. He never again showed me the love he had expressed in our past. Since I felt responsible for his emotional reticence, I figured I had to live with it.

I put my heart and soul into being everything he wanted me to be. Once my four children were born, I lived to a great extent on autopilot, but I was just surviving. As a young mother, my children came first. I didn't get to push and test my boundaries. Over the years I have heard from friends and other sources that if a person doesn't push their boundaries and explore their identity in their teens, it often surfaces later on as a midlife crisis. *I've come to believe pretty strongly that there's some truth to that.*

I loved being a mother. My children brought me so much joy and showed me so much love. I lapped it up and vowed never to repeat the mistakes (as I considered them) of my own upbringing. I allowed my children to freely express themselves. The children were included in most outings and the old Victorian notion of "children are to be seen and not heard" was thrown out the window. I did everything my parents didn't do and I thought I was being a fantastic mom by doing things 'my way'. My husband was earning a good enough salary to allow for my being a full-time mother, and since I had chosen to have so many children, it was my responsibility to embrace motherhood wholeheartedly.

I had a picture perfect life, or so it seemed. So why wasn't it enough? How spoiled did I need to be? Was I just bored? What was that nagging feeling of emptiness? I couldn't shake it.

Paul was happiest when I fulfilled his expectations of the role of wife and mother. He fully believed that if men and women maintained the old-fashioned roles of the past, there would be less strife in the world, and he projected those beliefs onto me. Over time I started doubting my own views. Recollections of my mother's pleasing ways left me destined to always think less of myself if I wasn't putting everyone else's needs ahead of my own. The difference between my mother and me, however, was that she truly seemed to be happy with her lot in life. I wasn't.

I began to realize that I didn't want to define myself in any particular way. I just wanted to be me. I wanted to be accepted as me, first and foremost, and not just as a wife or mother. And I knew that I wanted a soul mate. I yearned for someone who totally connected with me, who 'got' me. It frustrated me that Paul didn't seem to be that person.

I could feel his unhappiness with me too, not so much in what he said, but in his actions. He organized his life to make sure he could hang out with his friends and his colleagues, but made little effort to spend time with me. I was relegated to the back of the queue and my wishes came last. I told him on many occasions that I felt like I was his last priority. But he didn't take my feelings seriously. He thought that all he needed to do was take me away on a holiday, and that would fix everything. He thought that if he was able to have sex with me then things were all better. I knew it wasn't that simple. But I used sex to assuage him, to make him into less of a bear with a sore head, which he was inclined to be if I withheld myself from him. I used sex to keep the peace. Sad...but true.

I wanted to be closer to him. I wanted for us to act as a team where we were each other's first priority. I wanted the small, thoughtful considerations of somebody who cares for you. My heart was longing to find that kind of love. I wanted to reveal my innermost vulnerabilities and imperfections to Paul and know that I was being listened to. But I withheld my heart from him, and he withheld his from me.

Inside my soul was crying out for more! It was screaming at me to find myself, to be authentic, not to pretend any longer.

Eventually, I started listening to my heart.

The realization came in my thirties that I couldn't change Paul. He was too entrenched in his beliefs for transformation to occur any time soon. As my unhappiness in my relationship with him grew, I became increasingly happy with myself. I enjoyed being in my own company, needing him less and less. Instinctively I knew that even if I found my true soul mate, I wasn't ready. I had to change my own outlook to be happy. It had to start with me.

When my kids were at school, I used the quiet time to read, starting my journey with the words of others. I trawled the bookstore shelves searching for anything that "spoke to me". I read books which helped me work through my religious conditionings. I actually learned to like God—my God is about love, not fear. I read about past lives and karma and gained perspective from the injustices faced by so many people living in the world. For the first time it struck me: we are on planet Earth to grow. It is a school for the soul and we grow in our consciousness with each lesson learned. "The Invitation" by Oriah Mountain Dreamer got me through my times of greatest doubt:

It doesn't interest me
what you do for a living.
I want to know
what you ache for
and if you dare to dream
of meeting your heart's longing.

It doesn't interest me
how old you are.
I want to know
if you will risk
looking like a fool
for love

for your dream
for the adventure of being alive.

It doesn't interest me
what planets are
squaring your moon...
I want to know
if you have touched
the centre of your own sorrow
if you have been opened
by life's betrayals
or have become shrivelled and closed
from fear of further pain.

I want to know
if you can sit with pain
mine or your own
without moving to hide it
or fade it
or fix it.

I want to know
if you can be with joy
mine or your own
if you can dance with wildness
and let the ecstasy fill you
to the tips of your fingers and toes
without cautioning us
to be careful
to be realistic
to remember the limitations
of being human.

It doesn't interest me
if the story you are telling me

is true.
I want to know if you can
disappoint another
to be true to yourself.
If you can bear
the accusation of betrayal
and not betray your own soul.
If you can be faithless
and therefore trustworthy.

I want to know if you can see Beauty
even when it is not pretty
every day.
And if you can source your own life
from its presence.

I want to know
if you can live with failure
yours and mine
and still stand at the edge of the lake
and shout to the silver of the full moon,
"Yes."

It doesn't interest me
to know where you live
or how much money you have.
I want to know if you can get up
after the night of grief and despair
weary and bruised to the bone
and do what needs to be done
to feed the children.

It doesn't interest me
who you know
or how you came to be here.

I want to know if you will stand
in the centre of the fire
with me
and not shrink back.

It doesn't interest me
where or what or with whom
you have studied.
I want to know
what sustains you
from the inside
when all else falls away.

I want to know
if you can be alone
with yourself
and if you truly like
the company you keep
in the empty moments.[1]

My loneliness, I would later realize, was mostly a result of my lack of trust in other people. To truly expose your vulnerabilities, to be open, real, and raw, you have to trust in others as well as yourself. I had spent my whole life believing that staying closed off was the safest option. After all, the 'real' me was bound to face rejection. And therein lay my dilemma. Expose myself and risk rejection? Avoid rejection but never open my heart fully to another? I was young and foolish and I didn't understand that unless I loved myself enough to share myself completely, I could never really love someone else, let alone be loved by them.

The thing is, as soon as I began working on myself, I started attracting different people and situations into my life. I felt that there were so many people around me who never revealed their unhappiness, fought

---

1 By Oriah Mountain Dreamer from her book, THE INVITATION © 1999. Published by HarperONE. All rights reserved. Presented with permission of the author. www.oriah.org

against their souls' longings, and suffered in silence. And, in fact, I was one of them. I had created an image of what I thought I should be, and presented that for all the world to see. However, I was cheating; it couldn't last. Something would have to give, and something did. Ultimately the decision was taken completely out of my hands, for I was to meet a kindred spirit.

When Lara was introduced to me on a skiing holiday in La Plagne, France, we connected like old friends. I felt as if I had just met a potential new best friend. She was beautiful, with sparkling blue-green eyes and a charming big smile. She was naturally friendly, five years older than me, and had two girls and a husband.

We had so much to talk about. I admired how vivacious she was. I found myself taking note of where she was in the room and looking forward to seeing her after a day out on the slopes. We got to know each other in the evenings over dinner, with people having to pry us apart. We certainly had a friendly personal connection—but that's all I thought it was.

I remember the exact moment something changed for me. All the women had made a tobogganing chain, one behind the other, linking legs around each other's waists. I had linked my legs around Lara's waist, when suddenly time stopped. I could feel the stars descend upon us. I could hear my breath and feel my heart beating. I could feel the cold air on my face and prickles of electricity running over my body. My senses were alive and on high alert. Before I knew it, the spell was broken. But that moment remained in my subconscious.

We became fast friends, and when we returned to South Africa Lara called to arrange for us to go cycling together. We proceeded to cycle together regularly, both really looking forward to our daily sojourns. It was such an easy friendship; she made me laugh and being with her made me feel more alive and happier than I had been in ages.

Then one day I shocked myself; I was incredibly excited at the thought of meeting her for lunch—I even had butterflies in my stomach! Why was I so nervous? It slowly dawned on me, and when it did, there was no turning back.

I was in love with her. I was in love with a woman!

What was I to do? Did she feel the same way? How could this be happening? My brain rejected it over and over again, yet whenever I saw her, my heart confirmed it. My senses were heightened around her. I wanted to spend every waking moment with her. This was it—this was what I had been waiting for! I knew this deep in my soul. I had met my Anam Cara—the Celtic words to describe a "soul mate".

I was married with four kids. This would shatter their lives. How could I? How could I not? Would I continue living a lie or would I take the jump? I'd been wrong before, so how could I know she's the one?

It was at her husband's birthday party when we fully embraced our feelings for each other. The tension between us was palpable. Eventually many of the guests left and the kids nodded off, one by one. Then Lara and I were finally alone, toe-to-toe on the couch, staring into each other's eyes until it became too much. Lara got up, walked over, and gingerly gave me a small, gentle, lingering kiss on the forehead. I needed no further encouragement and literally threw my arms around her. I brought her close into me. It felt completely right. It felt natural, wonderful, and perfect.

Lara left on a trip after that night and we spent two weeks communicating by phone, falling deeper and deeper in love. On her return, we met on the beach and our fate was sealed. We were besotted. What next? How would we tell our husbands? We knew we had to be honest. There was so much at stake and so many people would be affected by our decision. But this was our truth, our reality.

When we confronted our husbands and children it suddenly felt like an unstoppable freight train. Our husbands did not take it well. Mine was more upset, or so it seemed, about breaking up the family unit than about losing me. He even suggested that I just see Lara on the side, keeping it a secret while continuing on with our marriage. Lara's husband exploded with rage and kicked her out of the house with nothing but her clothes, calling her a "fucking lesbian". Her husband's rage would abate, while Paul's was still to come.

The next step was to tell our parents. My parents took the news as well as could be expected. They were shocked, but despite being unsure about my decision, they said that they would always support my happiness because they loved me. I was so relieved. Here I was being less than perfect and they still loved me.

The shock waves were felt throughout our community and families. People were simultaneously horrified and intrigued. Some hedged bets that our relationship wouldn't last, that it was just a phase we were going through.

I realized very quickly who my true friends were. Much to my horror, I lost some friends whom I'd thought would be lifelong. They felt the essence of who I was had changed, because I was now a "lesbian". I had needed them to stand by me and accept me and help me through this transition, but it was not to be. Another lesson. From their rejection came the realization that true friendship must come with no strings attached. My true friends remain constant to this day.

Our children provided us with our greatest lessons. They all reacted at different times and in different ways. Again, these lessons were painful. My oldest son decided that he wanted to live with his dad. This broke my heart. My ego took a massive knock and the barrage of negativity I aimed at myself was endless. *I'm not a good enough mother. My son hates me. I've let him down. I'm a bad person.* It took some time before I realized that he needed something I couldn't give him at that moment. But I had to set him free. I released him with an open hand, hoping that one day he would fly back to me.

My two eldest children felt they had lost their mother. They felt rejected. My eldest daughter took on the role of mother, feeling like she had to pick up the slack. The lesbian issue was a source of great stress for them, as were the new rules of the house. Merging two families with different ways of doing things is no small task.

I feel that Lara has been the reward for my bravery. She accepts me exactly as I am. She has taught me how to communicate truthfully, even if what I have to say might hurt. She encourages me to have my own view and I have thus learned to love myself and how to properly love her. We complement each other beautifully. Neither of us is perfect and we like it that way. I finally have someone who gets me and I couldn't be happier.

My ex-husband and I finally divorced after a very bitter struggle. I have had to learn to own my power. The only things we can control are ourselves and how we see the world. I have had to let go of my self-imposed guilt at no longer fulfilling others' expectations of me, especially my family's. My marriage to Paul helped me discover much about my own strength. I have learned to be humble and compassionate and to deal with life in the present. I try not to project past issues into the 'now'. To see the world with new eyes every day and to react accordingly brings me the greatest joy.

I am still defining myself and working out my path. For that reason I don't think my midlife crisis is quite over. My 'unfolding' from a seed into a beautiful flower, wide open, embracing life with gentleness, humility, and awe, remains a work in progress. I am thankful to all those along the way who pushed my buttons. Without people to challenge our definition of self, how will we truly know ourselves? We do not know light unless we have experienced darkness. We do not know peace unless we have experienced discontent.

The 'mistakes' I've made have encouraged my soul's growth. Falling in love with a woman has taught me to be so much more accepting of others, how irrelevant gender is to the equation, and that ultimately, the most important thing in life is to love—especially oneself.

Journey to Myself

TRISH MITCHELL

At twenty nine, I had everything I had ever dreamed of: a truly drop-dead gorgeous husband, beautiful twin boys of fifteen months, and a newborn baby daughter. We were living in one of the most beautiful cities in the world, had a small but very characterful home in a great area, were surrounded by a large circle of friends, loving and support-ive families on both sides, and my husband had an upwardly-mobile career. We were, as my sister-in-law liked to say, "The Golden Couple." As I type this story, not even eleven years later, I am living on the same street, but my husband and I have been separated for just over three years. And it was my choice to leave.

So how do I explain what happened between then and now? How do I explain leaving an apparently happy marriage, ripping my children's lives apart, rocking our social world and devastating our families (and the aftershocks keep coming)? What gave me the courage to do what I believed was the right thing for *me*, despite the onslaught of advice to the contrary? Strenuous opposition came even from my grandmother who, at my father's funeral, told me that the stress he'd experienced as a result of my decision to leave my husband had directly led to the cancer that had killed him.

I guess the first niggling doubts about my marriage surfaced when I finally came up for air after my three children started preschool and I had three hours a day to think. Was this enough for me? Was just being a mom enough? I had stopped working when I became pregnant and had no intention of going back. I was all too aware that those Super Moms—women I knew who tried to do a good job of mothering while pursuing their careers—struggled with guilt that they weren't doing a good enough job at home, and that they weren't doing a good enough job at work. I didn't intend to fall into the same trap; we had agreed I would be a stay-at-home mom, and besides, we didn't need the money. I was prepared to give up using my expensive private school education and my university degree because I had always known I wanted to be a mom.

Around this time my husband's career was really taking off. He was working all day, attending dinner meetings, conferences and sports events, travelling internationally, and playing serious touch rugby to keep fit. Although by all accounts he is a truly good-looking man, he is not flirtatious and he isn't the type to have an affair. But he was in love with someone else: himself. And I felt left out. So I demanded more from him—more time, more love, and more attention. He responded by sacrificing the things he wanted to do in order to meet my demands, and it left him feeling desperately frustrated.

He had always struggled with his temper and we often had heated arguments, but now his verbal abuse escalated into physical abuse. While he never struck me, he often shoved me and exhibited other threatening physical behaviour. He bullied me into submission to the point where I stopped expressing how I felt altogether. Instead I would warn him, "If you carry on like this, one day I will just leave." He didn't believe me. He steadfastly pursued his own life, and left me to figure things out on my own. So unhappy, but understanding full well you can't change someone, I decided to find a therapist and change myself. It was one of the best decisions of my life.

Therapy certainly wasn't an easy path, and it didn't resolve my marriage problems. My husband didn't believe in therapy and wouldn't attend. But the most important thing I've learned about therapy is that it doesn't change you to suit other people; good therapy makes you a better version of yourself. That version, however, isn't always the one that people around you want. I became much clearer on what I wanted from my life and from the relationships around me, and I started to see where I wasn't being true to my own values. Therapy didn't make me easier to live with. It didn't gloss over the issues in our relationship. It did, however, start to clearly delineate which issues were mine to work through, and which ones were the result of two people with drastically different views trying to make a life together.

I still felt deeply conflicted about working. I didn't really want to work outside of the home. And while I have many interests and pursue them all, I didn't want to turn any of them into a career. The prospect of losing the freedom to be there for my children whenever they needed me was, and still is, deeply distressing. But deep down inside I felt imbalance in my marriage increase dramatically. I felt I was becoming less powerful, while my husband's power was increasing. The longer I remained outside the workforce, the less marketable I became, while my husband could devote himself to his career, increase his earning capacity, and still come home to a beautiful home and well cared-for children. My needs became less important, and he felt less inclined to accommodate them. After all, he knew I loved our lifestyle and our social life, and there was no way I could recreate that on my own.

We moved to a bigger house and put our children into private schools. I was still in therapy, trying to figure out what I liked to do and how to love myself. I tried to cover up the loneliness I felt, and take the pressure off my relationship with my husband, by taking up hobbies. Over the course of a couple of years I tried: decoupage; beading; scrap-booking; cross-stitching; photography; running a gift basket business from home; knitting; Pilates; cooking; reading; and journaling, just to name a few. My husband smiled benevolently on my activities, amused at my diversions, contented to remain ignorant of what I was discussing in therapy. He was quite happy with the 'new' me, who was keeping herself occupied with other things. It meant he didn't need to feel guilty about having his own life or preoccupy himself with mine. The romance of our earlier marriage was completely gone now, and he was under the impression that simply by living under the same roof we were 'spending time together'. It didn't make sense to him that he needed to keep proving his love nor did he agree that he had to make some kind of an extra effort to show it.

Then came the hobby that changed it all: tennis. I was invited by a friend to join in on a group lesson, and I loved it. I had played squash very seriously when I was at university so I was quite keen to take up a similar sport. Our coach was lovely—warm, thoughtful, encouraging and gentle. He spotted my enthusiasm quickly and asked me if I didn't want to start taking my tennis a bit more seriously. Absolutely! I started playing more and more and improved quickly. I soon outstripped my friends and looked around for fresh challenges. I stopped the group lessons (too frivolous) and started private lessons. I looked forward to them more and more. And then one Saturday morning it struck me: It wasn't just the tennis I loved, it was the time I was spending with the coach.

I decided I needed to talk to him about what I was feeling. My next tennis lesson was very early one crisp Saturday morning, and with my tennis racquet tucked under my arm, I stood on the court in a safe position on the other side of the net, and confessed that I thought there was more going on between us than just tennis. I was utterly taken aback when he confessed that he was deeply in love with me. He was married too, to a woman 16 years his senior, and had been unhappy for a long time. We contemplated our options. I agonised over the prospect of having an affair, but my honesty won the day. I couldn't face the thought of sneaking around. Three weeks later I left my husband.

My decision shattered our lives and, more importantly, the lives of my children. Friends and family tried to intervene in the most unexpected, direct, and confrontational ways. Someone (to this day I am not sure who, but I am told it was a 'good' friend) even phoned Coach's wife, ostensibly to share their feelings on the matter and also to tell her outrageously untrue stories about me. Several of the husbands in my social group went so far as to contact my husband and offer to get together a posse to confront the coach and beat him up! Coach received telephone calls threatening him. It left me reeling. Even three years later people are still trying to intervene. My husband, however, never once tried to fight for me.

From the beginning, he accepted my decision fairly passively. I think he could see I had made up my mind, but his passivity was unnerving. He shed a couple of tears, but he didn't beg me to stay, or try to convince me. He simply asked me if I really knew what I was doing. I can recall only one time where he 'reached out', sending an emotional text to my mobile phone, asking me if we hadn't had some magic at some point. His indifference shocked everyone else but me; it justified my leaving even more.

To this day I do not regret my decision. I made this decision to save myself. Selfish? Absolutely. But I can't live my life for my children, or for anyone else for that matter. This was the path towards growth. It took a huge amount of courage to fly in the face of my love for my children and my desire for them to have happily married parents. I endured the disapproval of all those around me, including my own parents—my father was especially concerned about my financial security. Many of my friends have not accepted my decision easily (if at all), and the repercussions for Coach have been equally strong. It has been stressful, traumatic, heart-wrenching, and deeply sad. But I remain steadfast in my conviction that it was the right thing to do.

Coach is an angel in my life. He is adoring, loving, and charming, with old-fashioned manners that leave me feeling protected, respected, and cared for. I have grown in ways I can't even begin to describe. He has built me back up brick-by-brick and shown me what a good relationship looks like. When I am with him I feel free to explore myself and my creativity, and to express my deepest longings.

I have an extremely amicable relationship with my husband—we live practically next door to each other. We go on holidays together, we go to dinner and movies with the children. We spend Christmas, Easter, and birthdays together, but the coach and my husband do not cross paths. This arrangement was not arrived at easily and has required tremendous flexibility, sacrifice, and maturity from all involved. Conventional, it is not.

Is this my happy ending? I wish I could say it was. I don't believe this situation is sustainable in the long run, for any of us. I am not divorced from my husband; that door is still ajar. Sometimes I think this is his way of fighting for me—by not closing the door. But despite the fact that he still loves me, he is still extremely disparaging of therapy, and in my view, that leaves us with few opportunities for reconciliation. Neither is my relationship with Coach perfect. He is not divorced, and I am not sure what our future together holds. The harsh reality of returning to the workforce looms large on my horizon—I will have to work whether or not I am with Coach, so that bridge will have to be crossed eventually.

So what have I learned? I've learned that you have to understand and love yourself before you can ask another to show you that love and understanding in return. You are responsible for your own happiness. You cannot live your life for others, because that's not a life. There are very few things in life that are truly black and white—just infinitely varied shades of grey. And in the end, it's up to you to have the courage to choose the colours that will saturate your life.

To Marry or Not to Marry: Is there a question?

NANCY CHAPMAN

Marriage is a three-ring circus–
engagement ring, wedding ring and suffering.
–UNKNOWN

Don't believe the haters. Don't listen to the cynics or the comedians, either. True love and 'happily ever after' doesn't just happen in fairytales. I've always believed that the world needs more love. Just think of how Prince William and Kate's fantasy wedding allowed the world to think about something other than the global recession and Gaddafi's troops marching into Tunisia for a moment, giving us the opportunity to whimsically ponder such things as beauty, pageantry, and Pippa Middleton's dress. I'm a romantic; I love weddings and always well up when I first glimpse the bride as she floats down the aisle towards her beloved. But now that I've reached midlife, I find there's a movement afoot amongst my peers that's challenging my beliefs on love.

When I was young and single, I thought that only cheaters divorced. And as I understood it, though not actually knowing any, cheaters were cowards who chose to hurt their spouses by finding a new partner

49

instead of working things out. But now that I'm in my forties and on my 15th year of marriage, I am starting to see relationships crumble all around me. And there isn't a cheater in the bunch. In fact, amongst the people I know, there's not been a single incident of the big 'As' at play in any of their splits: no adultery or abuse, no alcoholism, no one's even being an asshole! What has been happening is two lovers recognizing that they've grown apart, and admitting that they rather like it that way, or at least prefer divorce to a future of bitter compromises and unfulfilled dreams.

But amidst the inevitable ebb and flow that is married life, how do you know when that pendulum just isn't going to swing back anymore? Or perhaps even more to the point, in the heartache that ensues from untangling your lives, your children, property, friends, and money— why do we even get married at all?

Three-times divorced Frank Sinatra famously crooned that "love and marriage go together like a horse and carriage, you can't have one without the other." But while technological advances have allowed us to bid adieu to the horse-drawn carriage (they're expensive to maintain, stink, and leave giant piles of poop in their wake), society clings to the idea of marriage. Why hasn't marriage become as antiquated a notion as that horse-drawn carriage itself? Especially given that fifty percent of marriages end in divorce.

> *Marriages don't last. When I meet a guy, the first*
> *question I ask myself is: "Is this the man I want*
> *my children to spend their weekends with?"*
> – RITA RUDNER, COMEDIAN

The way we live today seems so dramatically different from how we lived long ago, or even during the time of *Mad Men*. Back then, unions between men and women were often economic. In the '50s, women were frequently valued solely for their ability to improve a man's life (sex at the ready, cleaning, cooking, child-rearing, assistance in climbing the social and corporate ladders). But while today's women are financially independent, might have babies before marriage, and keep their maiden names, for the most part they still want to believe they will spend the rest of their lives with Mr. Right, once he's (finally) been found.

But why? Women are smashing through glass ceilings, yet they'll still wait for someone to get on bended knee to pop the $25,000 question. Marriage is still a key milestone in Milton Bradley's The Game of Life. Divorce, however, is not.

Much to my grandmother's chagrin, at the age of twenty-three I left my boyfriend and went to graduate school 3,000 miles away. "No man wants to marry a woman with more education than he has," she said, wagging her finger at me. I met my husband getting my MBA.

But Grandma's warnings stuck with me. I didn't want to be the last one standing in life's game of musical chairs. At twenty-eight, I decided I was nearing my 'best before' date, and I wasn't going to wait any longer for my boyfriend to put a ring on my finger. I gave him a deadline to propose or I would be forced to look for Mr. Right elsewhere. A few weeks before our wedding, one of my best girlfriends held an intervention with me. "How can you be sure he's the one? Are you *sure*?" she demanded with her piercing you-can't-lie-to-me eyes. To be perfectly honest, I wasn't sure. I wasn't sure this marriage was going to last ten years, let alone forever. I just couldn't see that far ahead in my life. But the hotel was booked, and I knew that I wanted to spend my foreseeable tomorrows with him. I knew that much for sure. In order to quiet my fears, I pushed my girlfriend—and my cold feet—out the front door and locked it behind them. We were married within six months, in front of 250 guests and ten attendants, before dining on a surf-and-turf feast.

Over the next fifteen years I learned that a good, enduring, loving marriage takes work. Marriage is a lifetime of compromises and spending holidays with the in-laws. It's not always long-stemmed red roses when you least expect it, although they are lovely. It can mean sex when you're not really into it, or none when you are. It's crumbs on the counter, a sink full of dishes, and a mountain of laundry with smells and stains that are not your own. It's constant communication when things are going well, and cajoling, whining, yelling, and crying when it's not.

My husband and I did settle into a groove eventually. I cooked. He took out the garbage. I washed the laundry. He folded it. We both pursued our careers with abandon. When, three years into our marriage, we decided to get pregnant, I finally filled out all the forms to take his surname. Although it felt a bit like erasing my hard-earned past, I did it to create our future; it was important to me that we all have the same last name, like a team, and since our babies were going to have my husband's last name, I couldn't bear to be left out.

We wanted to have a baby before my eggs got any older (another painful 'truth' delivered with aplomb by my gran) and while on maternity leave, my consulting office shut their doors. So my slide into the shadows began with my open-ended maternity leave. Gradually, I'd evolved from a career-minded girl to a stay-at home mom.

First, you start taking showers while the babe is sleeping. If the baby doesn't sleep, you don't shower and you don't care. You don't want to have sex, you just want to sleep, and eau de spit-up is a useful deterrent. Your days are spent tending to the needs of the baby first, because that's what good mothers do, and you don't even realize you haven't eaten until you find yourself gobbling cold Kraft dinner uncovered while cleaning out the seat of the high chair with your hands.

Then you have another baby and there goes any chance of finding time to shower, so you hand the baby over to your husband the moment he walks in the door and head out for a run and a shower; that is, if your husband's not out networking or golfing with clients. Eventually the babes get to preschool, and you fit grocery shopping, folding a load of laundry, a 30-minute workout, and a shower into those two glorious hours by yourself! You might get into a new groove, making friends with the mothers of your children's playmates. Once in a while, you might even have a moms' night out.

Until one day you realize you're living your life amongst your family's leftovers.

You may have created a nice life with those remnants, but what could you have accomplished if you'd started with the whole shabang? Maybe

I wouldn't have to re-arrange the dishes after my husband loaded the dishwasher. Maybe the kids wouldn't always be yelling, "MOM! Where is my homework/backpack/favourite jeans?" Maybe when people ask me what I do for a living, I could say proudly, "I'm a writer," instead of mumbling, "I'm a stay-at-home mom."

About five years into my marriage, my husband and I went to the movie *About Schmidt*. In it, Jack Nicholson has a soliloquy that has haunted me for years. In it, he describes how, after forty two years of marriage, he began to question who the "old woman" was who was now living in his house. He finds himself wondering why everything she, Helen, does annoys him, from simply pulling out her car keys long before they reach the car, to cutting him off mid-sentence. He finds he has grown to hate how she sits, how she smells, and he vehemently resents the fact that she has forced him to sit on the toilet while urinating, despite his promises to always wipe the seat.

It stuck with me, because I don't want to become a 'Helen', but I worry that I already have. I yell at my boys when they don't put the seat back down, and I've grown suspicious as to why my husband keeps buying me perfume. When I look around at the older couples I know, it seems that many of them have stopped sharing beds, and even bedrooms, citing reasons of snoring and sleeplessness. What has marriage become for them? Are older married people just destined to wind up living like siblings? Is the alternative to divorce and remarry younger and have a daily multivitamin cocktail that includes Viagra?

One of my best friends is forty, beautiful, a successful executive, and has never been married. She handles prying questions (some covert, others not) about her sexuality with grace. She's an old-fashioned girl at heart, firmly believing that men should make the first move, but that they should not be intimidated by a successful working woman. Yet guy after guy has fallen short of her expectations. She finally went online last year, had a series of dates, and is now dating a guy she out-earns, and they squabble over money. She's planning a girls' trip to London in the spring, and can well afford her beloved Louboutins. He wants her to move in with him and start living on his limited budget, but I think she's lived the high life too long to be happy without it. Maybe the sex *is* that good, but what's the point in getting married in that situation? As blogger Veronica Kavanagh so bluntly put it, "Why buy the whole pig when all you want is a little sausage?" Especially since, by the time we are in our forties, nearly half of us will have become part of the divorce statistic. You have to wonder if *not* getting married is actually the answer to relationship longevity—case in point, Goldie Hawn and Kurt Russell (both had endured failed marriages before trying love without the wedding). Similarly, despite having so many wedding dresses, Barbie never did marry Ken.

So with all that said, why *do* we bother getting married? I've looked to own friends to try and answer that question. My more devoutly Christian friends who married young tell me rather glibly that they did so because they were horny. They got married so they could have sex with the blessing of God and their parents. But ask anyone who works at an ice cream parlour or in a candy store: once you have access to the forbidden fruit all the time, its appeal wanes significantly. And of course, the 21-year-old person you fell in love with is guaranteed to be markedly different than the 41-year-old person you are married to now, and even the religious ties that bind can't help every marriage weather those changes.

And then there's the 'whoosh' of passion explanation. It may be immature thinking to believe that if love feels so good in its onset, then marriage will capture those feelings forever, but it's certainly a recurring theme amongst my friends. Despite what Frank Sinatra croons, you can have marriage without love, just ask any recently divorced person about the last few years of their marriage. Aptly named, the 'whoosh' is that flushed thrill you feel when your lover enters the room. It is fleeting and certainly not capturable, no matter how much you spend on your wedding. The number of couples I know lamenting its loss and changing partners in search of it is testament to that. Look no further for an example of that than American woman Linda Wolfe, married twenty-three times (so far!). The self-proclaimed romance addict recalls her first marriage at the age of sixteen as the longest and happiest of her marriages.

Then there are the more base motives, those of money and/or fame. More strategic unions, where each partner gets something they want in return for marriage (usually backed by a strong pre-nup). How else would octogenarian Hugh Hefner land hot twenty-something after hot twenty-something? The economic incentive for marriage—like dowries in the forms of cows and chickens—has largely disappeared in the industrialized world, yet some women (and men!) still dream about getting an MRS ("Mrs.") degree, that most coveted wedding ring in lieu of an actual diploma at university, and never having to dirty their hands with work again.

Probably the most common reason, however, is that despite Greta Garbo's famous proclamation, people don't really "vant" to be alone, at least not forever. People possess a strong need for face-to-face companionship and enduring love. For both men and women, their greatest fear—over sickness, poverty, and homelessness—is being alone. Humans are a highly social species. Just look at our obsession with Facebook; it's obvious that most of us thrive on sharing our life experiences with other people. To know that you won't die alone is the pot of gold at the end of the rainbow for many a newlywed. And that companionship also presents a gateway to achieving hopes and dreams. It is access to a world that's easier and cheaper and, hopefully, more fun to experience as a twosome. It does feel wonderful to be on a team, to work towards a common goal, you have someone to confide in and to comfort you when the going gets tough.

But if your dreams grow and evolve to take you down different or even conflicting paths, can you avoid throwing the marriage 'baby' out with the bathwater? When the going gets really tough, can anything— be it a piece of paper, religion, or what have you—hold you together? And what about that thing of "staying together for the sake of the kids?"

A friend of mine believes that the moment you get pregnant, you should put yourself second (you'd take a bullet for your kids, without question), and that includes working on your marriage. But in midlife, when your kids are grown up and able to survive without you, where does that leave moms? Particularly stay-at-home moms who have given up careers and every shred of what they used to be. It leaves many wondering where the smart, vibrant, capable woman who attracted that man in the first place went? The woman who raised respectful, smart, contributing members of society: how does she define herself now? There has to be more for her than just shopping, going to the gym, chauffeuring the kids, volunteering, and waiting for grandchildren.

It is in this void that marriage often undergoes its toughest scrutiny. Faced with time to assess, renew, and rejuvenate, stay-at-home moms take their laser focus to their marriages and sometimes they don't like what they see.

A friend of mine just left her husband to pursue her dream of creating music. A friend of a friend left her husband and kids to pursue a life-long dream of training for the Olympics. Another woman left her husband and son to move closer to her parents, and she now visits her son just twice a month. These women are subject to gossip and judgment from all corners. Yet we know it's a double-standard. When men pursue their dreams it's said to be in the interest of the family, but when women do the same it's supposedly at the family's expense. What does this teach our sons who will have partners one day? More importantly, what does it teach our daughters? My own father still laments the fact that I am a stay-at-home mom, my hard-earned MBA gathering dust.

What if you discover in mid-life that you miss your old life and want it back? What if you thought the only thing holding you back from your fullest potential was your marriage?

What I've observed in my own sample size of "divorced-in-midlife" friends, is that in each of their cases one person's hopes and dreams were no longer compatible with their significant other's desires for the future. Not content with a future of the same-old, same-old, women in mid-life finally have the time to explore the life options they'd always wondered about. I don't judge these women; they are my friends and their circumstances are not unlike mine. Unwinding a marriage is heartbreaking and difficult, and I can tell you in no uncertain terms that their decisions were not entered into lightly.

Their experiences have shed light on my own midlife experience. I too have found myself asking similar questions. Do you remember when you used to look at your husband with such love it felt like your heart could swallow you? Or the moment you first laid eyes on each other on your wedding day, when your throat constricted and tears sprung to your eyes? Where the hell does that feeling go? When did you first notice that his nostril hairs needed trimming? When did he become deaf to your requests, or immune to your crying? When did his 'breathing' start to annoy you and keep you up at night? Somewhere, somehow, in midlife, the game changes. Kids appear, work distracts, metabolism slows, what we *should* do takes precedence over what we *want* to do, and the marriage takes a backseat to a mountain of priorities. Resentments simmer unchecked until hurtful comments stain the air or a kindness clears it.

But my answering of these questions has produced a different outcome from many of my friends. Love begets love they say, so I try to choose to be quick to love (and to communicate, and to hug). Just like we teach our children, it doesn't hurt to say, "I'm sorry." I make certain to say "I love you" daily.

My friends have caused me to re-think and renew my position on love and marriage. Marriage is work, there is no doubt, but there is beauty and value in that work and I cherish growing older with my partner. I would still choose him on a crowded dance floor, but I also don't fear the 'd-word' any more because I've seen that life does go on afterwards. And I don't believe people should be forced to stay together for all eternity, simply because you made a promise once when you were young. Life is too precious to waste. But I think in mid-life, when you're evaluating whether you're living your best life, take a good long look at the person beside you and remember that once, you utterly loved one another, and see where that thought takes you.

An Unexpected Opportunity for Growth

DEBORAH BRAUN

During the course of a year and a half of therapy in my forties, I felt the compulsion to write a book I was going to call *The Unspoken: What isn't voiced by the "lucky ones."* Well, in the summer of 2011 I turned fifty and still I hadn't written a book. Now that I've completed my Master of Arts in counselling psychology, I better understand my experience and recognize the value of "voicing" the challenges and rewards of my journey.

I married at thirty. My husband, John, was a striving young business-man when we first tied the knot. His efforts were well-recognized by his employer, a major national bank, and he was rewarded with various promotions and opportunities to relocate. We had met in my home city of Vancouver, then moved to London on a corporate transfer shortly after we married. A serendipitous conversation between my best friend and a customer at her rotisserie chicken restaurant provided me with a very beneficial business contact, and I began a small business within a few months of arriving there. My self-esteem and passion for my work flourished. I felt an inner contentment, a rootedness, and excitement for the travel, culture and adventure an international life offered; John and I both possessed a sense of wanderlust, so we indulged in any opportunity to travel across Europe and the UK.

Three years later I experienced the irrepressible urge to start a family. Fortunately, my husband did too and our daughter was conceived shortly afterwards. But alongside the joy of starting a family came a health shock. I thought that I might be having symptoms of diabetes: weight loss, outrageous thirst, and fatigue. At seven months pregnant I flew home for a vacation where I met with a local OB/GYN who noted high sugar results after a routine urine test. He sent me for a glucose test, the results for which were positive: I had gestational diabetes.

When I got back to London I underwent extensive testing. Because my glucose results were so high, I was prescribed insulin for the final months of my pregnancy, though I was reluctant to inject it for fear of falling into a diabetic coma if my glucose count fell too low. Along with fear, I felt anger, confusion, guilt, disappointment, and loss. I was sick, unable to control my own well-being, and dependent on medication. I had been robbed of the carefree experience of eating what I wanted, when I wanted. Fortunately, as soon as I gave birth, my blood sugar levels returned to normal. While my newborn daughter Jessica's hovered distressingly low for the first few days of her life, after an extended hospital stay we both went home healthy.

My transition into motherhood was very smooth. I felt a deep love and strong bond with my daughter and I felt physically and emotionally supported by my visiting parents, eager husband, and helpful friends. One early spring evening, John enthusiastically described a flattering recruitment call he had received from a highly successful, well-paid colleague at a New York-based investment firm. While I felt excited for him, I felt this would represent a loss for me. I had a visceral reaction in the form of a thickening in my gut and a knot in my throat. For the first time in our marriage, I sensed that my husband's goals and dreams were not aligned with mine. But he was our breadwinner, and he had always supported, encouraged, and revelled in my professional growth and success. I didn't believe I could hold him back from exploring what might be the career offer of a lifetime. I stifled my disappointment and allowed myself to be romanced by the lure of wealth and the many benefits it might bring. Once he was offered the position, we shared our news with friends, relatives, employers, and clients. However, I had felt a deep sense of fulfillment with the work I was doing in London, and so I began to quietly mourn its loss.

The QE2 was our indulgent mode of transit for our return to North America, and we spent our first month in Manhattan before settling into our first home in a leafy suburb. The busyness of motherhood and resettlement distracted me from missing my working life, but I did miss spending time with my husband. Along with his high salary came long hours (up at 5 a.m., home at 8 p.m.). I had become the 'trailing spouse' of a successful career man. I met plenty of other moms in similar situations but I just didn't feel a strong connection with them. Frustrated by the monotony that sometimes comes with parenting a young child, a lack of variety in my friendships, and a homogeneous blur of housewives, brokers, and lawyers—I started feeling disconnected from my husband's life. Our needs differed: he was tired and overwhelmed by social interactions and pressure at work and needed time to decompress at the end of the day, whereas I craved social stimulation and a strengthening of my connection with him.

Without realizing it I, like many new moms, was letting Jessica and John's needs supersede my own. And that's when the depression began. I just didn't have the energy to swim, or run, or do anything at all to take care of myself. I wasn't lacking sleep, but I found myself starting to nod off while Jessica napped during the day. I called my close friends in London and Vancouver less and less. I'd treat myself to expensive haircuts and clothes in an effort to make myself feel better, but that led only to me feeling guilty and even more disconnected. Fortunately when I became pregnant again that depression lifted, at least until the last trimester. Then the gestational diabetes returned alongside the feelings of frustration about my lack of energy and restrictions to my diet, not to mention the fear that I might become diabetic for the rest of my life. But I felt enormous relief when I gave birth to a healthy son and the diabetes once again left my body.

We moved to a bigger home and I enjoyed some creative expression while redoing the house but a year later, when the decorating was complete, I felt my mood drop once again and my bitterness rise. This time, I felt low in the morning. I'd wake up feeling unprepared to cope with the stress of the kids, afraid of making decisions. My favourite foods tasted bland; I started losing weight. My resentment towards John built. I felt hurt, neglected by his work, and I wanted his fun-loving energy to help my boost my spirits. I envied his freedom, and the excitement and stimulation of his career life. Because he knew he didn't deserve my anger, and he probably feared he was losing his formerly enthusiastic wife, he tried in his 'guy' way to straighten out my perspective. A few times he got angry and told me to just "get myself together." That just made it worse, however, and I stopped sharing my pain altogether. Our kids were fine, but it was a rough time for us. A close friend later shared that she'd felt like just "breaking up with me." Apparently, I was being really negative—certainly not the encouraging, inspiring executive coach who had once thrived in London.

I was too embarrassed to talk about the depression and anger with anyone. I continued to stuff away my discomfort and mask the symptoms. Of course, it oozed out in angry outbursts at my husband, impatience with our children, and fatigue and frustration in general. During a dinner conversation with my best friend on a trip home to Vancouver—a talented and caring nurse—I got up the courage to talk about the grey zone I'd been struggling to get out of. I told her how food tasted flat and just plain chewy, that I wanted to sleep way too much, that I was full of self-criticism, and that I had moments of relief but kept feeling low. She told me that it sounded like I was depressed. As I digested her concern, relief washed over me. Someone understood, and wanted to help me return to my old self. But then she started with the "anti-depressant medications can really help" advice. I knew she was earnestly trying to help, but meds, really? Nope. I told her I'd talk to my doctor, but didn't disclose that I felt diminished, even irritated by her suggestion of medication.

Shortly after returning home from Vancouver I was scheduled for an annual check-up with my doctor and shared my depression concerns with him. He frankly shared his scepticism of therapy, but gave me the contact information for a psychiatrist. It wasn't until late that night that I mustered the courage to tell my husband about my concerns. He was surprised that I felt depressed, and reflecting on that now, I can understand why. I had hidden my challenges, and like many people he hadn't recognized my withdrawal as depression. A few days later, I booked an appointment.

The therapist's office was in an upscale community, and my first impression was that she was one of those practitioners who prescribed 'happy pills' to privileged housewives. Yes, I was living a privileged life, but I yearned to understand my emotional struggle, not sedate myself with medication. Surprisingly, my therapist never discussed medication. Instead she encouraged me to challenge some unfair and idealistic expectations I had of myself. The experience of having someone hear my story, ask insightful questions, and demonstrate genuine concern helped validate and normalize my distress. But I was still challenged during this period.

After my husband had chosen a golf work trip over a romantic getaway, I took another trip home to Vancouver to lick my wounds. During this trip, I came the closest I have ever come to cheating on my husband. I knew if I expressed my sexual interest, a close friend would have opened the door to make it happen. Fantasizing about it both excited and scared me. It rocked me that I had been capable of even considering cheating, but I also realized that that trip was a catalyst for me. I started to realize that I had put aside my needs while placing an inappropriate emphasis on supporting my family's interests. I was fortunate to have two healthy children, a loving husband, and want for nothing, but I still had the right to grieve the lives I'd left behind in Vancouver and London. At the urging of my therapist, I finally allowed myself to acknowledge those losses and that I was doing less of what made me happy...and that was making me miserable!

Therapy helped me to ease the perfectionist tendencies that had rendered me impatient, self-critical, and anxious. I learned to share the sadness that had fueled my anger towards my husband, and to voice requests for support, which I had previously considered weak or indulgent. The journey was a tough one. It was uncomfortable to examine myself so closely. But after a few months I felt more confident, pursued friendships with other like-minded people, spoke more assertively, and felt more alert and appreciative of the beautiful place I lived in and all the joys of family life.

My midlife journey faced another setback that summer, however, when a chance visit to a GP revealed the return of a health menace. The diabetes was not gestational this time, it was type 1.

The thought of living the rest of my life as an 'ill' person was something I felt absolutely unprepared for. Yes, having to inject medication several times daily scared me, but it wasn't just that. It was also about seeing myself as less-than-healthy—as someone others would pity. That no matter how hard I tried, I would remain unhealthy. I felt powerless, mad, sad, very scared, and very alone. I lived among healthy, intelligent, outgoing people. How would I fit in? Who could relate to my situation?

John was out of the country at the time, so I called a friend who has suffered for years with chronic fatigue. She let me cry, and quietly listened as I shared my anxiety about feeling different from others, and tried to soothe me as I catastrophized all the scary complications of diabetes: loss of sight, limbs, mobility, and quality of life. As I did this, many pieces of the puzzle started to come together. Diabetes had made me feel tired and less vibrant. Coupled with my perfectionist tendencies, depression, and unfair expectations of myself, I had become angry inside, and old before my time.

A few months later 9-11 happened. Life around Manhattan changed, and my health concern seemed insignificant in comparison to the losses of others. The following year John was downsized and when he told me of a potential job offer in Vancouver, I gathered the courage to voice my wishes. I felt enormous relief and love and respect from him when he put his energy into securing the job. Fortunately he got it, our house sold quickly, and a year after his downsizing, we loaded our Westfalia van and set off on a cross-Canada family adventure. As we covered the thousands of kilometres of expansive, varied, beautiful countryside of our homeland, reuniting with family and close friends, swimming in lakes and prepping meals outdoors, my anxiety melted away and my heart began to sing again. My life with chronic illness was beginning to educate me, and I needed to pay attention. And although I still had alarming sugar lows, my physiology was responding positively to my growing inner contentment and with it, my crisis was lifting.

In 2005 I returned to school and earned my graduate degree in counselling psychology. Clearer in my values with respect to family, health, creative endeavours, and balance. I paced my studies out over four years and practiced easing my perfectionist tendencies. I've specialized my practice to assist people in dealing with their own chronic illnesses—helping clients manage their distress, get motivated, and build skills and healthy self-care routines. It's been tough. Sharing my story at lectures still chokes me up. Telling others I was depressed is uncomfortable. But when people tell me it helped them to hear it, my courage grows. To help others feel better about themselves, ease up on unfair expectations, live truer to their values, and manage stress or depression in healthy ways has been an honour. Little did I know that my midlife crisis would so positively influence my career, help me get closer with my family, feel more love for my husband, appreciate his respect and support, and find a way to be a role model for living healthily with a chronic illness.

I'm now fifty-two. I've been living ten years strong with type 1 diabetes. My lifestyle has remained exactly the same as before my diagnosis. I exercise moderately with thirty-minute swims, hour-long dog walks, hikes with pals, and bike rides around town. I continue to enjoy a delicious range of foods. Ever since the diagnosis, I've never hidden my needles. I don't have something to hide. But I never label myself as "diabetic." This illness doesn't define me. It's just one element of my life.

My midlife crisis was triggered by a cluster of transitions: an agreed-upon but not chosen relocation from the UK to the US; shifts from part-time, self-employed stress management coach, to part-time mother to full-time mother; and an unexpected progression from gestational diabetes to type 1. I had felt guilty for not deriving as much satisfaction and happiness from my life as others. But today, I have far more appreciation for just how lucky I am. I'm more resilient than I previously thought, my commitment to health keeps me feeling good despite—heck, *in* spite of—a chronic illness, and I no longer compromise myself. I've developed a more realistic perspective overall, and that has been essential in moving forward. I won't lie, the journey hasn't been easy. I could have skipped the depression, and I still wish I didn't have diabetes, but I am grateful. And ironically, I feel like a healthier person than I ever was before.

The Great Skate

L. FLETCHER

At forty-seven, I fessed up to the fact that I've been experiencing varying elements of a midlife crisis for the last eight years.

I remember clearly a bright summer morning when I woke up, at thirty-nine years of age, and asked myself in a blur of semi-consciousness: *What am I doing? Who am I? Is this what I wanted for myself? Is this happiness?* I knew that I had, in that instant, opened the Pandora's Box of great existential queries of midlifers the world-over. And now that the box had been opened, it had released a gnawing little gremlin that would not go away. I managed to stall the gremlin by keeping myself busy with my social life and doing everything I could to support everyone around me. I became extremely adept at putting myself last. My daughter, my husband, my job, my family, my friends, my home, even strangers—everything and everyone came before me. Because as long as I was doing everything for everyone else, I wouldn't have to face my own life.

That worked for a couple of years. Intermittently I would become conscious of my dodging, and I'd try to fix it with a flurry of hot yoga and massage sessions, or a trip or two on my own to some exotic country for some 'me' time. When that didn't really do the trick, I'd chalk it up to the fact that I was about to turn forty-two, and one was *supposed* to have some kind of crisis at that time, wasn't one? I started to look at the choices I had made that had brought me to this place.

I started with my choice of husband: a lovely man, hard-working, clever, devoted to his children, wise and funny, but also at times nasty, petty, negative, and distrustful. I did not feel special with him. I felt distant, lonely and separate. There was the neighborhood we had chosen to live in: a West Coast neighbourhood nicknamed the "Canadian Riviera." It was beautiful, exclusive and sought-after, but really, it was pretentious, supercilious, and full of people I could not relate to. The food we ate: only organic and from Whole Foods, Capers, or Urban Fare. I looked at how I was choosing to rear my child. The school: French immersion, *mais naturellement,* and a private tutor. Her extracurricular activities: soccer, piano, skiing, and dance. All the trappings to raise the 'right' kind of child, one who would thrive in a world to whom access was privileged to just five percent of people in the world. I even started to look at the friends I had accumulated, and my relationship with my family. ALL of it. All the trappings I had bought into, that I had willingly surrendered to, and which bore no connection to who I actually was. Why had I accepted them so readily? Where were my own beliefs in all this? Was I a human being or a human doing? The more I looked at my world, the more critical of it I became. And the more critical I became, the more I shut down.

I became a master at recognizing all the crap, but I was a complete failure when it came to actually dealing with any of it. Instead of getting therapy or counselling to do the real work needed to get to the heart of my blossoming crisis, I kept shoving it deeper inside, deluding myself into thinking the issues I was raising would magically disappear.

I began what I describe as "The Great Skate." I started skating through my life on a thin layer of self. All the hard-to-deal-with memories, all the hurt and pain that I had accumulated throughout the course of my life were festering away underneath a veneer of superficiality; all those trappings had nothing to do with the real me. I had no interest in my marriage or my body until the former had totally disintegrated and the latter had begun falling apart. My head was so full of self-loathing that I could not even look at myself in the mirror. My feelings had even begun to manifest physically, and looking at the weight I had gained in recent years left me spewing vileness and negativity at my reflection.

I let old friendships lapse because I considered anyone who was connected to the person I used to be a threat; they knew how far I had fallen. I was too screwed up to maintain friendships in a meaningful way. Sure, I'd have a boozy lunch with friends every once in a while, but only so long as conversations stayed far away from the truth. I knew that close family members were nattering away, gnashing their teeth and wringing their hands with worry about the bad shape I was in, literally and figuratively. They were right to worry, but my self-destruction continued, going on and on...for years.

Then one day I saw a girl walking down the road with a friend. I had probably seen girls like them a thousand times. They looked so at ease. So lovely, free, and spirited. I yearned to be that person again. I was so far from being her that I could no longer remember what it felt like, and it terrified me. The world I had constructed around me was a fortress of discontent. I saw it clear as a bell and I could no longer hide my true feelings. Intense sorrow spilled over onto everything I did. I was so sick of my life, and myself, that I had a complete and total breakdown. I cried for four days straight.

Enough was enough. I had to do something.

I dealt a crushing blow to my marriage by telling my husband that I felt our relationship was in an abysmal state. That there was very little real love there, and so much distrust, anger, and discontent that I could not take another minute of it. I was miserable and needed to make a change. We discussed breaking up, but decided instead on intense therapy, two days a week, to see where it took us. We would do it together at first, and then each of us on our own. The couples' therapy lasted just a few sessions. We basically spent the entire time going through our history together and grazing over what brought us to that place. It was a safe place to air grievances, certainly, but it resulted in few changes once we left the room. Our counsellor suggested we'd be better served by working on ourselves. My husband continued the therapy for a while, but then he had to leave the country for work, so I continued going on my own.

For our first solo sessions I spent a lot of time divulging my inner thoughts, prompted at times by her questions. It went on like that for a while, the process allowing me to unburden myself. Then the real work began, and I started to actually listen to myself and what I was saying. I had to look at my own bullshit—the heaps and heaps of it. I'd used so many excuses not to deal with the issues that were at the core of my current problems, some of which dated back to my childhood. I had never properly dealt with my mother's death from breast cancer when I was going through puberty, nor the radical self-reliance I'd had to develop in order to cope with her five-year-long illness, and the ultimate loss. In addition, my father's stern, stoic way of parenting left me feeling as though being vulnerable, or really opening up to anyone, was never an option. I was a virtual fortress, trying to control everything, including my emotions. I had to go through many layers of painful memories and deep emotional work until I could reveal the truth—and the worst was yet to come.

By therapy session eight I was in 'How did this all happen?' mode. I had a pretty good man for a husband, a beautiful, spirited daughter, a great home, a bevy of loving friends, a supportive family and an enviable career in the arts. Given the quality of life experienced by the vast majority of people in the world today, what right did I have to be so self-absorbed? By the tenth session it had become drudgery. I was disgusted at myself for letting things get so out of control, for being such a coward, and wasting so much of my life. By session twenty-four I had gone through sadness, elation, pity, anger, loathing, fear, angst, back to elation, sadness, hope, anger, curiosity, elation, all the way back to mourning, then finally, some acceptance so that I began to look at myself with more compassion. With each session I was deconstructing and reconstructing ways of looking at my life. It was chaos. But then something really wonderful happened. I came to understand that I am on a lifelong journey towards understanding who I am truly meant to be: my authentic self.

During this process my husband was very supportive, but yet unwilling to drill down into it with me. At the time I had appreciated the space, but as I look back I wish he had been willing to embark on the journey with me. While I was doing this work, he too was working in his own way. His journey, while completely peculiar to him, was similar to mine in many ways, and it's why I felt we should have been undertaking far more of it together. He was sensitive to my subtle changes, my moods and my new ways of communicating; he gave me a lot of room to grow which meant a lot of 'space'. Because of his job we spent a lot of time apart, living almost parallel lives. Therapy exposed a gulf in our 'togetherness' that had suited me initially, but ultimately did not represent the type of relationship I desired. We came to realize that being intimate soul mates for life requires greater daily invest-ment than either of us had been making. We are in a much better place now than where we were, and I trust him completely, but we are not terribly intimate or passionately close. I do not have a burning desire to share every little bit of myself with him and sexually it is more 'off' than 'on'. I sometimes wonder if that sentiment is representative of many marriages (it seems to be amongst 'the ladies' of my wine-fueled lunch sessions). Perhaps it is more common than anyone is willing to admit. But we do share really lovely times. We genuinely like spending time together (just not lots of it) and we share frequent good laughs. I can tell he enjoys my company and that, in turn, makes me feel more secure.

After six months of intense therapy, I had learned that most people in the world go through some kind of transition in their midlife. For some, it resembles a crisis, for others, an awakening or a searching. And unless they really allow themselves to experience whatever it is they are facing, they will be unable to transition to the next phase of their life. Fear is a major obstacle when struggling to find one's 'true' self. For me it meant going back to the very beginning of my life and working my way forward. I had to throw away endless reams of inse-curities and personas I'd created for myself to mask my very lonely and somewhat damaged childhood, one that had set the stage for my own self-reliance. A childhood that shunned vulnerability and celebrated ironclad coping strategies. I had blazed through most of my life never really revealing who I actually was as a person, never truly opening up myself to anyone.

I realize now that I have actually been "skating" since I was a kid, but only in midlife, beginning that morning at age thirty-nine, did the ice beneath me begin to crack. It was then that I began a slow drift into unmanageability, finally forcing me to face the issues I'd been avoiding for decades. And although it took a bloody long time to face them all, it has made the foundation on which I now stand deeper, broader, and stronger. It may be the result of being older and wiser and just 'getting over' whatever I was going through, or it could be that I burrowed into the depths of what I saw as my worst self, and found out I wasn't all that bad.

I am still endeavouring to be more conscious about who I am, the help I need, and the life I desire. I am more prepared to mine the well of humanity, and embrace the things that truly make me whole and happy. I trust that I will be on that journey—if you can call it that—for the rest of my life. I've stopped my official therapy for the time being; at the moment I don't feel as though I need it, but at least I know it's there if things get sticky. I no longer skate through life, and I'm getting better at accepting all the elements of my identity, including my faults, fears, joys, and vulnerability. I still struggle with sharing all those elements of myself with the people I love, and have come to accept that I am naturally a person who keeps their own counsel, I am not sure more therapy will change that. The marriage may or may not last, but I am committed to being as real and honest about where I am at as I can be, and there is way less drama as a result. I am better equipped to make choices for myself and my family as I enter into the next phase of my life, clearer and more confident now than ever before.

Mid-Life in a Youth-Obsessed Culture

ESTHER KANE MSW, RSW, RCC

As I write this, I am about to turn forty-one, an age that I am surprisingly 'okay' with. I cannot say I felt okay about turning forty last year, as that particular birthday culminated in what I now most definitely consider a midlife crisis. As a psychotherapist for women, I am somewhat ashamed to admit that it took me at least quite a while to realize that I was even *having* a mid-life crisis, but luckily, I get paid to help *other* women through difficult periods of life, and not my own.

Lately in my practice I've been seeing countless women between thirty-five and forty-five years old who are experiencing full-fledged, no-holds-barred, downright nasty and merciless mid-life crises—a virtual tsunami, in fact. For men it tends to happen later on, around forty-five to fifty-five. That's the decade when a lot of long-term married men kind of 'lose it'. You hear stories of them running off with much younger woman and becoming party animals—regressing to their rebellious early twenties self, even getting giant tattoos plastered on bodies, frequent sources of regret later on when they come to their senses. I have heard an amazing array of stories with fascinating variations on the same theme when it comes to men. But let's return to the matter at hand...

Women are no strangers to craziness while in the throes of a midlife crisis. We get dangerous plastic surgery procedures performed on various parts of our bodies, overdo the Botox, have wild affairs, ride across the country on a motorcycle, or even adopt more children after our own have fled the nest. While the details of each woman's experience vary, the common thread seems to be that they are feeling a seismic shift within themselves that leaves them feeling lost, disillusioned, and even wondering who they are. They're often scared and confused and don't know where to turn for help. Inevitably though, when I suggest that perhaps they are in the midst of a midlife crisis, they often laugh and say, "I'm too young for that—that doesn't happen until you're fifty!"

I can completely relate to this way of thinking, I was convinced of the same thing too, until I felt that my whole life was turning upside down around my fortieth birthday a year ago. Nearing that milestone, I started to question every seemingly sound decision I had made up until that point. Even those that had previously given me great joy, stability, and peace. During the course of a single day, I might ask myself:

> *On being married:* Do I like being married? Why did I get married in the first place? What's the point of being married? Why do so many people do it? What would my life have looked like if I'd remained single?

> *On children:* Maybe I should have a child? I never wanted children, but maybe I have missed out on something fantastic and should try it out just to see.

> *On work:* Being a therapist is hard work, maybe I had another calling. Is my career just the result of a dysfunctional childhood? Should I have studied interior design instead? What if I was meant to be an interior designer and missed the boat?

On friends: Why is this person my friend? Do I even like him/her? Does s/he even like me? Did I choose this friendship because I thought I couldn't do any better? Did this person choose me and I'm just going along for the ride? What do I really want in a friend? Have I ever had a really good friend? What kind of friend am I?

On where I live: Why did I move to this godforsaken island and leave big city life? I don't belong here. But I don't belong in a big city. Where the hell *do* I belong, anyway?

When I try to pinpoint when my midlife crisis officially kicked off, I would have to say it started when I turned thirty-five. My husband, Nathaniel, and I had met while both living in Vancouver (I had just completed my Masters in social work at the University of British Columbia), and were finding it really tough to make ends meet in the most expensive city in Canada. We had reached what we considered our 'financial peak' living in the city. We owned a two-bedroom condo and could just barely pay the bills, even though we were both decently-paid professionals. We hated condo life as well as being in the middle of a bustling city where we had to fight for good work, so we made the move to a small community on Vancouver Island. Life there is much more affordable, slower-paced, and financially sustainable. We have both done well at setting up our businesses, and they are thriving. It took a while for us to find like-minded friends, but it happened slowly and overall, we've both been very pleased with the move.

I should also point out that we are a Jewish couple who consciously chose not to have children when we first met (I have known I didn't want kids since I was in my twenties). This was very tough on us for many reasons, but primarily because of the pressure we felt from our families to have kids. It was made very clear to us that we had deeply disappointed them with our decision, and that was hard to swallow and move beyond. We were openly shamed in a way only Jews can manage, with comments such as: "Too bad I'll never be a grandmother. I was so looking forward to it [*long sigh*]. Oh well. I guess I'll live."

Then everyone our age started having kids en masse. We have now spent over a decade 'losing' our close friends as they built their little families. The losses for both of us have been huge. The worst was when my best friend in Toronto had two kids, one right after the other and everything changed forever. She never had time to talk on the phone, never came out to BC to visit (even missing our wedding) because it would be too expensive and she didn't want to leave her kids. Even though we feel we definitely made the right choice by not having kids, it's been extremely difficult fitting in with our friends who now have little ones running around. And we don't blame them—child-rearing is all-consuming and there's not much time left for friends at the end of the day when you're looking after little people all the time.

For most of my childbearing years, my husband and I were judged harshly for openly admitting we didn't want children. Many people called us selfish for not wanting to raise a family and this hurt us deeply. We thought it would be selfish to have children that we didn't really want. It wouldn't be fair to deny them the time and adoration they wanted/needed because their parents weren't all that into child-rearing. But now that we're moving out of our childbearing years, it feels like a huge weight has been lifted because people have, for the most part, stopped bugging us about reproducing, and seem okay with our decision even if they don't totally understand it.

The end result of this decision was extreme isolation and loneliness and questioning how to fill my time without children meaningfully. Because of our decision we were often unintentionally pushed out of certain social circles due to lack of commonalities. That was the situation it had come to when I turned thirty-five. I had accomplished so many things to that point: finished two degrees with honours; met my husband; gotten married; started a serious profession with a lot of responsibility and stress; moved from Toronto where I'd lived all my life to BC; moved from Vancouver to Vancouver Island; bought a house; and opened a practice and gotten it up and running. But then the dust started to settle and I started to feel really uneasy.

All the other women I knew in my age range had many accomplishments similar to mine and were also raising children, though they were absolutely run off their feet. I felt they didn't have the luxury of indulging in thoughts like, *Am I happy? Is this how I wanted my life to turn out? What else do I want? Why do I feel so lonely and unsatisfied?* Luckily, I had (and still have) a wonderful connection with my husband and we have always had a solid relationship. I think it is precisely because I had this foundation that I was able to comfortably question certain aspects of my life without fearing losing him or what we had. Conversely, I think it is because we have such a wonderful relationship, that I sometimes questioned the whole child issue, because I knew in my heart that we would have been good parents. When everyone around you is questioning why you aren't having children, it's hard not to question yourself!

I tried my best to have a positive attitude and decided that I could put my 'mothering' energy (which most women my age were putting towards actual mothering) into my work; I managed to write three self-help books over the course of two years while working full-time as a therapist. I enjoyed writing and the fact that I could help more women via the written word, as opposed to helping just one person at a time in therapy sessions. I was doing press for the book and travelling extensively as a result, which was all thrilling and fun. But still, I felt an emptiness gnawing away at me all the time.

I was really good at working hard, yet not so good at slowing down and doing things simply for the pleasure of it. So I started going to hot yoga three to four times a week (still loving that). I took up knitting (and subsequently joined a weekly knitting group, which I really enjoy), and most recently, I've learned to play the ukulele, and joined a weekly community "uke jam" which makes my inner child beam.

I've realized that learning to have more fun—and committing to doing that regularly—is important to my overall well-being. I think it's an ongoing journey, and we continually come back to questioning our own happiness and quality of life as we age. I'm okay with that because I figure that as long as I'm questioning, I'm still growing as a person and that is more important to me than encountering a little emptiness here and there.

I've also worked really hard at making friends as a child-free married woman and it's slowly happening. To my great delight, I met a lovely gay man in his fifties at my knitting group, and we (as well as our husbands) have become great friends. We have so much in common: no kids, decent incomes, animal 'babies', and time to go out and do fun things together.

It's taken me roughly six years to find my footing and to feel the great mid-life fog lifting. But I'm definitely feeling lighter, both mentally and physically. I am pleased that I have made some good friends and found hobbies I find fun, challenging, and energizing. And while I'm not sure if I'm completely out of the woods yet, I do feel more confident in my ability to handle my inner angst.

Not Myself

TERESA

It would have been really helpful if someone along the way had explained middle-age to me like they had puberty. Back then, I'd read the books and I'd felt ready to be a teenager. Even when I became a mother, I felt like I was at least able to *try* to arm myself with some information on what it would be like, emotionally and physically, to be a mom. And I know that there is a phase in my life yet to come called "menopause." Granted, no amount of information, books, or support groups will completely prepare you for the experiences of growing older, but at least it helps knowing that you are not alone in it. So given the wealth of information on all these other significant moments in a woman's life, when I began to experience a resounding emptiness in my mid-life, I assumed it was a rare occurrence, that it was "just me."

It hit me around 2006 when I was thirty-seven. I'd lost the sense of fulfillment I'd felt in my twenties. It wasn't to do with my marriage, or children, or finances, or any of the more typical issues people reasons associate with sparking a midlife crisis; it was something deeper. I wanted an inner peace, a sense of knowing who I was and that I was doing something successfully, something meaningful in my life. Coming out of my twenties, I had felt comfortable and confident in myself and my roles. I was a teacher at a top-rated school and I felt like I was making a difference in my students' lives. I was part of an innovative program that integrated disciplines—the first of its kind in our area. I was creative with my assignments and the students and I enjoyed learning together. I presented at national workshops and even worked to help other teams create new courses.

I also worked with amazing people; I had peers that I could trust to give me feedback and support. We would go out for drinks and solve the world's problems together. In the midst of my professional success, I married the man of my dreams, the best friend of all best friends. We would hike on the weekends and spend hours just talking. We would fly out to San Francisco for long weekends and escape to a bed and breakfast at least once every few months. We both worked a lot, but we played a lot as well. It was a fun life, but after a few years of that, I was ready to start a family.

I knew I wanted to stay at home with my first child as soon as he was born. I enjoyed teaching, but this was one life upon which I stood to have the greatest biggest impact of all! I also didn't know how to be a great teacher and a great mom at the same time, so I put my career on hold. But as with any major life change, comes disruption!

The 'mom' world was very different from my professional world; it took some getting used to. I didn't take long for me to feel like I wasn't good at it. I'd always felt I was doing a good job as a teacher, but I didn't feel the same way about motherhood. I was constantly getting advice—not the helpful, "why don't you try this" kind of advice, but rather the "you're doing it wrong" kind. The conflicts and opinions over how I should be raising my child left me feeling inept. As my son grew older and went into his Terrible Twos, I felt bad that he didn't sit and listen like the other kids. Other parents kept commenting on how "active" he was, which I took to mean, "Why can't you control your child?"

I went from being in a profession where I was successfully controlling a group of thirty teens, to a position where I questioned if I was even feeding my family the right foods. I was happy being a mom, but I was not confident in what I was doing. I was pulled between advice from experts, my mom, my in-laws, and my own instincts. I questioned everything I did.

The flood of input didn't apply just to parenting, either. I felt insecure about everything I did. Being an at-home mom seemed to invite suggestions from others about what I should do with every moment of my time. Despite everyone giving lip service to the idea of parenting being "the hardest job of all," everyone seemed to think that my entire day should be filled with activities. Working friends envied that I now apparently had all this time to work out. So I hired a personal trainer and worked out at least three times a week. Helpful aunts implied I should do something creative, like crafts, to occupy all this 'free' time I supposedly had. Crafting raised my blood pressure far higher than teaching teenagers ever had. My husband volunteered me to work with the parent association, thinking it would help me to meet new people. So I raised money for the school, which felt good, but it was just organizing, nothing intellectually challenging. What I've since realized is that ultimately, I did all these things because I felt guilty. I wasn't doing any of these things because I wanted to. It wasn't out of passion or desire, but out of guilt over the fact that I was getting to stay at home with my sons. People said I should be doing these things because it was what *they* would have done if they'd had extra time; I was fulfilling their dreams not my own. And living a life according to someone else's vision, was whittling away at my identity.

My husband noticed and during a walk one evening he said, "I'm worried about you. You don't seem happy."

I was shocked! My brother had passed away a year earlier, but I felt I was doing well. I wasn't as happy-go-lucky as I had been when we first dated, but I didn't hate my life. My immediate reaction was to get defensive, but I held back and listened instead.

"You don't seem to enjoy things as much as you used to. Each day seems about the same to you. You get sucked in to worrying about things you can't control. You blow a tiny mess on the floor all out of proportion. You seem like a distant friend—you're not quite yourself," he said nervously.

I didn't speak. Instead I looked into his eyes and saw fear. He was afraid that it was him I wasn't happy with. For a while I wondered if that wasn't true. No. I won the lottery when I found him. Was it motherhood? I didn't feel totally competent, but I was starting to trust myself and my instincts more than ever. Was it the death of my brother? No, I was happy he was no longer in pain.

Wasn't quite myself. Was that the truth? Who was I anymore? I honestly didn't know. The more I thought about what he was saying, the more I realized he was right. It was as though I was living a life on cruise control, just going through the motions of living. I had stopped enjoying the small pleasures in life. I was nervous about being a bad mom, and it had preoccupied my life. I felt intimidated by women around me that seemed to be able to do it all, work, family, volunteering—they looked like virtual saints.

I moved through an internal checklist. We had just relocated from the Northwest to the South, maybe that was it? My knee-jerk reaction was to say "Well, *you* moved us," but it wasn't true. We'd been very deliberate about making the decision together. We'd each made a list of things that we were looking for in the perfect place to live and raise our family; his list wasn't more important than mine. We'd spent two years visiting five cities before buying an acreage in a city that fit us perfectly. Back when we were first married, I'd never have imagined moving away from our family and friends, but here I was, not missing family even though I was 1,000 miles away. I was not the same person I was back then. I was now part of a marriage and family, and I realized that those were the roles that defined me now.

I began to remember the craziness and unease I'd felt when I was pregnant, eight years before my brother's death and the big family move. I'd been diagnosed with a mild case of postpartum depression after my youngest was born. How I was feeling now was a lot like I had been feeling then. But back then, I'd thought there had been physiological reasons for it. The more I read about women and depression, though, the more I felt compelled to talk with my doctor. I wasn't crying every day or feeling like I didn't want to get out of bed, but I really didn't feel like I was living a meaningful life. So I went to see my doctor. She asked me a series of questions, took some blood tests, and eventually diagnosed me with mild depression.

I started counselling, which helped, but I found a practiced regimen of prayer, meditation, and journaling brought clarity to my thoughts even more than the meetings with the psychologist. I really did believe in my heart, that staying home with the kids was the most important job in the world. I began to see how I felt guilty for being able to do something so many moms could not. I began to see I was being pulled in every direction by the people around me, and each one of those directions was a reflection of their desires, not mine. I began to view my daily life with a new perspective.

With the help of a light anti-depressant and personal introspection, in a matter of weeks I started to feel differently. I started to find happiness in everyday life. I was more objective. I could see I was doing a good job as a mom and wife. I stopped overreacting to my kid's imperfections and celebrating their achievements. Instead of being overwhelmed by all the advice I was getting, I began to make lists of things I wanted to accomplish or felt strongly about. I started eating better and seeking out the sun, both of which made immense differences in my well-being.

But as my physical and emotional state improved, the time I spent in quiet prayer made me realize that I needed to confront the spiritual questions I was wrestling with; there were lingering issues that kept creeping into my mind during those quiet times. Over the years, the same question had been on my mind, but I always disregarded it. Now I felt that I needed to know the answer before I felt comfortable living in my faith and passing it on to my children: *Was God loving?*

I was ten when my father died. I'd been told that God only took good people, that his death had been God's will. They told me that God would never burden me with more than I could handle. But I didn't know how I felt about a God who takes a father away from a child or burdens her with the pain of loss just to see how she deals with it. I also lost my sister and then, years later, my brother. My family was gone. And while I had believed in God my whole life, I wasn't sure how the concept of a loving God fit with my own experiences. Did He love others and not me?

I began to look at my religion closely. I studied what the documents of my faith said, especially about the "Will of God." I was astonished to discover that, contrary to what people had told me, my church did not believe that God "took" people. When I realized that God wasn't out to get me, I began to look at my losses differently. Prayer and a new perspective also made me see that I had been given a great gift. I was so fortunate to have the relationships I'd had with these three, amazing people. I needed to stop being the suffering victim to whom all bad things happened. I needed to look at what a gift it was to have the father, sister, and brother I'd had.

Time and time again, reflecting on the things I was hearing from people around me, I was shocked to see that a kindred friendship with a sibling was rare, and my sister had been my best friend. And unlike many other people who have passed, I have never heard a negative comment spoken about my dad. His family and friends seem to feel his absence acutely even years later. I was given the best example of love from my mom and dad's relationship. My brother, who had suffered from addiction for years, was now free of his pain. All I'd ever wanted for him was peace, and he now had that. Page after page, prayer after prayer, revealed that my relationships with my loved ones had been unique. The truth is that if I hadn't loved them so much, their deaths would not have brought me so much pain. I began to be thankful for the pain I felt, because it meant that they had been special, that the love we'd shared was special.

What have I learned through my mid-life experience? Mainly that I need to take care of myself both physically and emotionally. I have stopped seeing change as necessarily a negative thing. Life changes, our bodies change, our roles change—sometimes for the better, sometimes not. In fact, instead of looking at this period in my life as a crisis—something I just needed to get through—I have begun to embrace it as a journey towards discovering new facets of who I am. I had been thinking of my new identities as wife and mother as representing losses, as though something had been taken away from me. I felt others were judging me as lazy and simple-minded because of my decision to 'give up' my career. Now I look at my new roles more as phases of development, like parts of a lifecycle. Some change is physical, some is emotional...but all of it is part of experiencing life. Oprah Winfrey once said, "Turn your wounds into wisdom." I have taken the wounds of insecurity, guilt, and pain, and used them to help me discover a better version of myself.

As a preteen, reading all the books on 'growing up' I understood that uncertainty and self-discovery were part of growing up. Once I became a grown-up I thought that the lessons ended there. I know now that life is part of an ongoing process of learning and revelation. In the next ten years, I will enter menopause, say goodbye to my children living at home (that is, if I've done things right), and there will no doubt be more transitions and more uncertainty. But now I'm at peace with that prospect and I look forward to the changes the universe has in store for me.

Unravelling

CAMILLA JOUBERT

I knew I had hit rock bottom as I lay in a fetal position on my walk-in closet floor crying uncontrollably and shaking violently. The bizarre thing was that in that moment I felt as if I wasn't in my body and that I was looking down at my physical self, wondering what the hell was wrong with me. Like a three-year-old in tantrum, I eventually settled into convulsive sobs and then abruptly stopped. I cannot imagine how long I lay there on the soft, wool carpet in the semi-dark, staring cata-tonically at my shoes which lay at eye level, neatly arranged accord-ing to colour, heel height, and style. How lucky they were to feel like they had order and function! My cherished wardrobe, bag, and shoe collections, things that were once important to me--were so utterly meaningless now. Who had I become? I was completely lost.

I would walk around having snippets of conversation, shopping, washing, feeding, cleaning, but I wasn't present. I had managed to 'exit' my body. It felt like even my soul had decided it didn't like being inside me! There was a massive void in my life and nothing could fill it.

For a long time before feeling lost, I'd felt stuck. Stuck in a life I felt I had little say or control over. That feeling of being trapped inside my head had been as visceral as the feeling of being lost and outside of my mind and body. The heaviness of it all made me feel like I was swimming through mud with the daily grind, and the endless, boring housewife duties that I trudged through. How had I gotten to the point of accepting boredom and complacency? Life was so predictable: our annual holiday to a family resort that we had been going to for eight years, our mid-week date. The repetitiveness of it all was picking away at the fabric of my being, thread by thread––unravelling me. I yearned for something to change, for the unexpected, for the element of surprise, for my husband to announce we were going to Europe, even with the whole family. But the logic of why we went where we went, was always drummed into me and no matter how passionately I wanted to be adventurous, there were other lives to consider. How could I *escape* the ordinary when the ordinary was what he desired?

Other than the fact that I was perhaps going insane, the only other conclusion I could draw was that I had to be having a midlife crisis. But at thirty-seven, how could this be?

If a stranger were to ask me what had brought me to this point, I might be stumped at what to answer because I couldn't pinpoint it then, and I still can't, even as I've moved beyond it. I could say it was the four family deaths in a span of two years, the demanding new puppy that came into our lives, the too-long nine-and-a-half week vacation stay of the in-laws, or the sudden realization that I didn't do things for myself on weekends, that I was not passionate about my work, at all, living vicariously through Facebook posts, or that I was just feeling bogged down by trying to survive the worst winter in seventy-five years! I had lost the joy for life.

I Googled 'midlife crisis' and came up almost empty-handed; even Wikipedia at that point had virtually nothing to say on the matter. I raced to the local library and armed myself with every book I could find on the subject of a midlife crisis, or anything vaguely close to the subject. That's when reality struck. I personally couldn't find a single book that suggested a midlife crisis could start before forty. It usually referred to women nearing their fifties who experienced empty nest syndrome and dull marriages they'd hung onto past their due dates. But what does a mid-life crisis look or feel like for a 35 or 40 year-old? Why does our society talk so little of this episode in younger women's lives? I became more frustrated and divulged my predicament to a close friend. She confided that she too had felt that way once as she neared her forties, until she discovered that she may have been entering peri-menopause.

Armed with more evidence, I had a series of blood tests done and swore to my husband that my behaviour was surely due to a hormonal imbalance! But I never really believed it, and when the results came back everything was disappointingly normal. Could I not blame something or someone? That was what I needed: to apportion blame and excuse away my overwrought, layered feelings of loneliness, irritation, boredom, fear, confusion, oddness— the list went on. The media had been doing so much to make peri-menopause a condition, and menopause almost a disease, that I was certain I'd be able to excuse all these feelings away as some kind of hormonal imbalance. But if only life were really so simple.

The feeling of madness was creeping up daily and I couldn't bear the thousands of thoughts running around in my head that I couldn't quiet. I hated that I was such a wreck of emotions and that I felt so directionless. I was incredibly uncomfortable with myself. I thought perhaps it was feeling devalued. I had a part-time business doing corporate promotion, but it was tedious and the value I gained from it wasn't enough to sustain my weakened self-esteem. How was I going to get rid of this self-destructive state? Months passed and waves of strength and weakness ebbed and flowed. The tumultuous blend of the two threw me into a frenzy of irritation as I battled to make sense of myself. Flashes of insight would thrill me for a few days and I would be resolved that all was calm and orderly. And then as suddenly as they came, they would all fall away.

I started to journal daily out of desperation. It was a release to put something--anything--down on paper, even those emotions I thought were ridiculous for me to be experiencing. Justifying each reason for my breakdown and building a case as to why I might even need to leave my husband, abandon my ten and seven year-olds, and go live in Italy where I could be surrounded by art. I was screaming for independence and craving culture. I was so desperate for a change of pace. My boredom with life was palpable.

I was so tired of being self-indulgent and caught up in my own mind. I desperately wanted to feel healthy again. Guilt swathed over me for a few weeks; how could I sit in my beautiful home, go for coffees, surround myself with wonderful, diverse friends, go for forest walks, and be so bloody unhappy? I think that was actually the first step to realizing that this was my current reality and that I was indeed allowed to express my unhappiness. I was not sitting in a mud hut in Africa or in a shantytown in South America. My needs were entirely different from people without the basics, but that did not diminish my feelings of unhappiness, and guilt wasn't helping me change my state of being. I'd always thought I was one of those people who was so in touch with my life and my feelings; I was supposed to be the 'happy one'. Friends always referred to me as "positive and happy" and my husband thought it was my best attribute. But I was not, and it was okay for me to finally admit it. I had been a 'people pleaser' for so long, that I was afraid to express my own desires, and that fear was holding me back from moving forward.

As I explored the issue, I could find mountains of information blaming myself, but a nagging sensation also sadly allocated some portion of blame to my marriage. Our lives didn't mesh together well any more, even though from an outsider's perspective it appeared as if it did. The function worked, my feelings didn't. But more profoundly, I felt like *I* didn't fit with my life any more. I felt like while I was something 'to' and 'for' everyone else, *I* was nothing. I had no sense of self-worth and value. I understood that I was bored and unfulfilled and that *my* dreams had not been listened to *for years*, and I resented it.

I especially resented the fact that my husband did not see or experience my pain. It was "my problem." But I was married to him—he was part of the problem. He was part of *my* problem. So it was *our* problem! But where had the teamwork we'd had early on in our marriage gone? He kept trying to "fix" *me* with endless suggestions of hobbies and activities that would occupy my time and, I suppose, distract me from the real issues. But it wasn't about *me,* it was about *us.* I couldn't figure out how long it had been since I'd felt I was in control of myself. I recognized that I had felt weak and powerless for a long time. The financial control he had in our family life had spilled into other areas of my life and I heard myself saying to girlfriends "I'm *allowed* to go with you." It shocked me to understand how afraid I was of asking to do things on my own. I would get heart palpitations just thinking about doing an activity on the weekend that did not involve my family or my husband. The imbalance of power needed to be addressed.

It was very important for me to make decisions about my relationship based on fact and not purely on emotion. I had seen too many friends evaluate their relationships on the basis of passion and the idea of being in love. I watched their relationships deteriorate because they thought being in love was the barometer to a healthy relationship. During this time my understanding of what was "me" work and what was "us" work became more clear.

I look back on that painful couple of years and wonder if it could have gone any differently. It was painful for everyone around me too; my husband didn't know what had hit him. His wife went from being a methodical, sane person who loved to talk a lot—in fact the brunt of many jokes in our family and amongst friends for this attribute—to an introspective, quiet, non-communicative person. Looking back, I'm sure that my introspection came from a need to try and cope with it all. Because I knew that the only way I could start to understand who I wanted to be was by tearing that 'old' me down and starting all over.

Finally I decided to explore therapy as a way of helping me disentangle myself from all these realizations. I spent weeks deconstructing the various patterns of behaviour that were harming me and my relationships. I recognized the choices I made along the way and how they affect me today. It was a long, arduous challenge to sit with feelings without them going anywhere; they were not going to surrender or easily accept the place they were floating around in. They had become comfortable! Only when I gave up trying to figure out my feelings, did it seem they finally started to fall away, one at a time. I was able to gain clarity by being in those darkest moments and surrendering to the situation I had found myself in: that of crisis and awakening. It is in those dark moments when you are working on your inner being—doing the "soul work" of seeking your destiny—that purpose often appears. And when I seemed to understand that I was growing and expanding my thinking and my sense of what was important to me, I ceased being as obsessed with trying to work it all out.

What I think a lot of women feel—and I am no exception—is a desire to find the time to be introspective about their situation. If you have children, it seems that they have endless needs: school commitments, challenges, sleep problems, appendicitis, H1N1, earaches, tummy aches, headaches—and on and on. Apart from the physical ailments, the psychological juggling is tremendously challenging. At one point I felt like committing myself just so I could have time to think! Selfishly, I needed to look at myself, and carving out that time was essential. It's pretty basic: finding the time to simply *be* and allow that wash of feelings to happen, only occurs when you make that time. It's a bit like grieving—you cannot get through the pain until you put in the time and effort to do it properly. It is a slow process and it cannot be shooed away or glossed over—it took me a few years to truly get over the death of my father, who died quite suddenly from a brain hemorrhage. It involves letting go of your old self while discovering your enlightened self, and it is a gritty process that is both exciting and scary. It is very much like the metamorphosis of creatures in nature that shed their exterior shells; the newly formed skin of those that have sloughed off their old layers is tender and exposed. Yet the vulnerability of that exposure, while frightening, is exciting in that it offers a world of possibilities for the future.

I could not relate to women who found pleasure in cooking or cleaning or ironing, or who, like the Dalai Lama, could simply be grateful for the small things and find happiness in doing so. Only when I really started to look at the emotional and physical steps I could take to change what I was uncomfortable with, did I see that I could carve out my own path. Instead of living within boundaries that someone else defined for me, I was free to set my own.

After some months of deep self-discovery I announced to my family that I was going to take a trip to Italy, by myself. It seems easy enough to simply express one's needs, but it was one of the most difficult announcements to make. I didn't ask permission: I made a statement. It was something that absolutely had to be done. My husband would have to cope with the kids, their schedules and school commitments, and all the extra curricula. My first realization was that I didn't want to do a trip with anyone (and I didn't want a hook up with an Italian hunk). I just wanted some dynamic time for myself. I needed to fill up my emotional tank, stare at the Sistine Chapel, catch trains, eat pasta, and be free to steer my own course. It was not a trip to find myself as Elizabeth Gilbert did in her *Eat, Pray, Love* experience; I had already found myself. This voyage was a gift to myself––a gift acknowledging that I had done the work to know myself and figure out what I valued most in my life.

I recognized the need for my soul to experience nurturing that came even from the simple things—art, travel, learning, biking, just going to the movies—and to express my new-found freedom, and self-reliance. The process prompted me to trust my inner voice, my intuition. To realize that I have a right to be heard, and that my life needn't always be about pleasing others—that pleasing myself is just as important! Ever since I recognized that, making decisions has become easier and I feel less guilty about making them. I know now what I am willing to accept and what I am not, which has been tremendously enlightening. Some days are better than others. I continue to make new discoveries about myself and each one supports my soul and brings me increasing inner peace.

I've oriented myself towards supporting myself while helping others, and I work hard to strike that balance. Half the journey to healing myself was coming to grips with the damage I had done to myself for not voicing my needs for so many years. My husband hadn't realized how overbearing and controlling he had been our entire lives. Neither had I. It was a slow awakening. I resolved anger through therapeutic talks with my husband, fear by finally expressing my desires, confusion by recognizing my role as a mother as being important even if I didn't get paid for it, sadness by recognizing my need to value myself and have others do the same. I have also learned just how important my friends are to me, but also that I had cast my friendship net too wide. Those most important to me were not being given their due, and less meaningful friendships were draining me. I drew my net in, and today I have far healthier friendships.

As tumultuous as it all was, I am grateful for my *unravelling* because going through that pain caused me to pause and reflect on every aspect of my life. My experience forced me out of an unhappy comfort zone and pushed me to reevaluate my situation and embark on taking steps to improve myself. Now I choose to live a life where I am present in ways that support my new ideals, goals and values. These discoveries have been the most meaningful of my life. I know *I* matter, which is why I've resolved to listen to my own voice and follow it, wherever it may lead me...

CPSIA information can be obtained
at www.ICGtesting.com
Printed in the USA
LVOW11*0825110517

534120LV00001B/1/P